Psychotic Remodeling

*True Stories From A
Serial Remodeler*

A How-Not-To Guide

Psychotic Remodeling

True Stories From A Serial Remodeler

A How-Not-To Guide

Rick MacKay

Pulpville · Denver

Psychotic Remodeling

"Humor is emotional chaos remembered from tranquility"

- James Thurber

Psychotic Remodeling

Printed in The United States of America.

Second Edition

ISBN 0-972-9233-0-6

Library of Congress Catalog Card Number 2003094779

Cover Concept: Author

Interior Illustrations: Rick MacKay and Travis MacKay

Design and Layout: Andrea Sommer

Portions of this book originally appeared in *Fine Homebuilding* magazine, June/July 1983, No. 15 (Fixing a Leak); and *Fine Homebuilding* magazine, August/September 1984, No. 22 (Spraying a Ceiling).

Newspaper clippings **"Mississippi Man"** and **"Man, agitated by washer, fires 3 shots into machine"** originally appeared in the *Rocky Mountain News.*

Excerpt from **"Mr. Blandings Builds His Dream House"** granted courtesy of Turner Entertainment Co.

The events portrayed in this book are true. Most of the names have been altered or disguised to protect the innocent.

Table OF CONTENTS

Psychotic Remodeling

*For Kathy, who believes in me and puts up with me
at the same time.*

Psychotic Remodeling

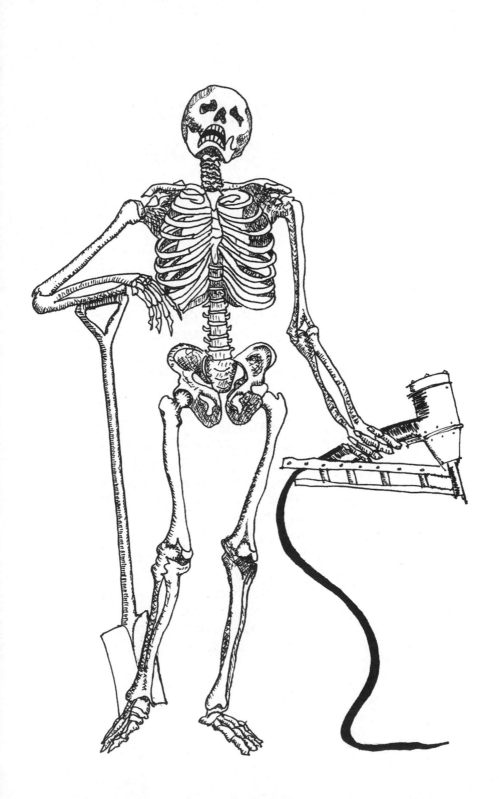

Mississippi man shoots plumber, family, kills self

Associated Press

JACKSON, Miss. — A man who was enraged over house repairs shot and wounded a plumber, his own wife and his son before killing himself.

Police found Bentley F. McKinney, 77, dead in a back bedroom after storming the man's tear-gas-filled house on Monday.

McKinney shot plumber Roger E. Cliburn, 52, then shot Gertrude McKinney and their son, Burt, authorities said.

A person who worked with Cliburn escaped without injury.

The plumber, who was wounded in the right shoulder, was treated at a hospital and released.

Gertrude McKinney was in stable condition with a head wound and her son suffered a critical stomach wound.

McKinney "was despondent about some repairs being done to his plumbing," said Deputy Chief Bracy Coleman.

Introduction
MISSISSIPPI MAN

Tear-gas and evening mist mingled in the pines, circling the old Victorian tucked into the woods. The 911 call came from the plumber's helper, Billy, a husky youth in his first week on the job.

The lucky apprentice was fetching parts from the truck when he first heard gunshots, then screams. He hesitated for a long instant, torn between helping his boss and saving his own ass. A second volley of gun-shots and screams sent him racing across the road to the neighbor's.

Mrs. B___ was watching "Matlock" and was oblivious to the carnage across the road. She nearly jumped out of her house dress when Billy pounded on the door screaming bloody murder. Living across the way from Mc___ for 30 years taught her he was an ill-tempered sonofabitch. For the love of God, he even shot her dogs for trespassing. What with Billy's gasping and pointing over his shoulder like that, she knew the twisted old fart was up to no good again.

Fortunately for the plumber, a Sheriff's deputy was patrolling nearby. Within minutes three units had surrounded the house, and the plumber crawled out of the front door under the blare of a bullhorn. From a stretch-er he told the deputies Mc___ was holed up in the back of the house with a gun. He wasn't sure, but he thought the old man's family might be dead.

Authorities reached Mc___ within the hour, a suicide victim in the corner of the back bedroom. Had he not kept the police at bay with rant-ings and potshots, his son might have survived.

A thorough investigation by the Sheriff concluded there was no wrongdoing on the plumber's part. The old man just snapped.

I've hired this plumber many times; you may have, too. He probably came to fix something that had to be done right away – a busted toilet, leaking water heater, or, worst case scenario, fix something started by the homeowner. Maybe the plumber was compelled to bring the old plumbing up to code. He is distinguished by his ability to turn a $200 visit into an invoice of $2,000.

Because of the emergency nature of the call, he may have showed up after hours – a euphemism for time and a half.

Perhaps the Mississippi Man's water pressure was zilch, the switch in his pump went out for the hundredth time, out-of town company was on the way, and his water pipes were hopelessly constricted with rust. From his bedside he called a plumber, water feebly coursing through his house like the blood of a heart attack patient on life support.

If the house was old enough, the piping would be as brittle as a widow's bones. One bad pipe after another, the threads rusted in their fittings, would crumble beneath the steel teeth of the plumber's wrench. A one or two hour job was dragging on into the middle of the night. And although the plumber was now charging upwards of $100 per hour, there was "no way" he could predict when he'd be done. Or, the final cost.

Holes were appearing in the ceiling at the rate of three or four per hour as the plumber searched for fitting after fitting, plunging his saw into the lathe and plaster. Patches would cost $50 each, and there were nearly a dozen – not to mention repainting. A flimsy plastic tarp, full of holes, was spread over the new carpet for "protection." Plaster dust filled the air and pea-sized chunks of the stuff collected in the gap between the baseboard and the tarp.

"When will you find the leak?" Mississippi Man kept asking.

"There's no way to tell. We're doin' the very best we can. That's all I can say."

"You've been here for hours!"

"I can't help it!" the plumber argued. "When the water starts to goin', it just runs all over the place." He pointed from one corner of the room to the other. "Just 'cause it's drippin' here don't mean it ain't leakin' there, sir!"

Maybe the plumber had the audacity to take umbrage at the constant questioning. Water still trickled through the pipes, mixing with the plaster dust and congealing on the carpet.

"How much more pipe do you have to tear out?" Mississippi Man wheezed. If he had his health, he would have yelled.

The plumber looked him in the eye and jabbed a stubby finger in his face. "I could shut this thing down tonight and re-pipe the whole house next week. Is that what you want? You just say the word."

The smell of age-old rodent droppings spread through the air, poisoning the house. A fine layer of dust covered the dresser and nightstands. The bedding would have to be washed and changed before they slept there again. Mississippi Man's emphysema was bad before – now it was worse.

His breathing came in short raspy gasps. The vein on his forehead bulged. "How are we going to clean this up?" he demanded.

Company was due tomorrow.

Perhaps his wife began nagging him to take control of a situation he had no control over. Powerlessness and frustration beget violence. It's possible the plumber was tired too, and ill-timed words were exchanged. Maybe that handgun by the bedside should have been kept locked up. Maybe Mississippi Man should have known what he was getting into.

Psychotic Remodeling

DEFINITIONS

Definitions

Psychotic.
A condition of the psyche or mind. Any kind of mental derangement or affliction which cannot be ascribed to organic lesion or neuroses.
Oxford English Dictionary.

Psychosis (pert. to psychotic).
Any mental illness, whether neurological or purely psychological...which renders the individual incapable of distinguishing reality from unreality or fantasy.
Concise Encyclopedia of the Sciences.

Psychosis.
Mental disorder... characterized by... hallucinations and delusions, severe mood deviations, inappropriate mental responses and severe distortions in judgment.
Concise Columbia Encyclopedia.

Remodel.
To make over; to rebuild.
Webster's New World Dictionary.

Dementia.
A species of insanity characterized by failure or loss of mental powers; usually consequent of other forms of insanity...
Oxford English Dictionary

The loss of the ability to reason.
Concise Encyclopedia of the Sciences.

Psychotic Remodeling

1 REMODELING DEMENTIA

A large remodeling project will typically cost as much as a new car or a small yacht. Consumers entering into such a major transaction in the real world will examine the merchandise, negotiate a price, secure everything in writing, and enjoy their purchase from the first moment of delivery.

No one in their right mind would consider having their "major purchase" built in their home. But for a moment, imagine you're a homeowner dying to make that major purchase.

Consider constructing a 20 foot sailboat in your living room. You would have to knock out a couple of walls, tear out the ceiling, and probably the roof, to accommodate the mast and keel. You would have to construct dust walls to isolate the boat project from the rest of the house. Wiring, plumbing, and heating would have to move, and the framing, drywall, and insulation would have to be removed and replaced. The kids? They'd go into the basement for five months.

Hundreds of workers would trudge through your home during the course of the project, beginning around 7:00 AM most days. Expect them to be sawing, pounding, and using all sorts of toxic sealers and finishes. Oil may leak from beneath their trucks, and nails will fall out of the beds of their trucks.

Framing and trim crews will arrive on the jobsite with truckloads of electric saws and air tools powered by noisy, breaker-tripping compressors. Most floor finishers require 220 volts for their drum sanders. Special electrical requirements for sub-contractors rarely make Do-It-

Yourselfer's Action Lists.

If the thought of a hundred strangers parading through your doors alarms you, and if you possess certain boat building skills already, you may decide to do the project yourself. You will save a great deal of money at the risk of losing your mind.

Doing it yourself also tends to skew the schedule. A task that might take three men one week, or 120 "man" hours, somehow manages to take a single individual 240 "man" hours, especially when fitted around work, family, friends, and fun. A Do-It-Yourselfer-Driven job can easily drag out long enough for infection to set into the psyche of an unsuspecting homeowner. Homeowners running the project themselves should expect that their personal life will go into the toilet for a while.

But Do-It-Yourselfers planning a home renovation project should beware: Before any soil is turned over or plaster is busted, there will be a few items you'll need to consider, including but not limited to pin surveys, soils reports, preliminary design, foundation design, structurals, interest rates, covenants, energy efficiency, construction financing, architectural review committees, scheduling, letters from your neighbors, building permits, zoning, lien waivers, engineering, landscape design, contingencies, liability insurance, workman's comp, preliminary meetings with a divorce lawyer (if married), and a note from your parents, depending on the size and scope of the remodel.

Do-It-Yourselfers should allow enough time and money to get these sometimes aggravating but required items in order. The only special requirements are time and patience and the ability to marshal the talents of dozens of trade professionals.

(If you live in a big city, you may think the local building department's mandate is not to promote public safety, but to test your patience. First time remodelers acting as their own contractor should rely on the building department for advice. They can be a valuable resource, but don't expect them to do your job. Inspectors will check the pitch of a sewer pipe in a basement, for example, but may not ensure that the soil it is bedded in is properly tamped.)

The sub-contractors that have bid your work expect the floors and walls will be level, plumb and square (if the construction is new) when they walk on the job. If they have to shim or brace or correct work by a previous crew, expect them to charge more than their original bid.

Reliable contractors or project managers routinely take care of these annoying details, and their fee is usually collected in the "overhead" portion of the bill.

Overhead is a percentage of the total bill, ranging from 15% to 100%, depending on the complexity of the project and the anticipated red tape.

Obviously, a simple basement finish will have a lower projected overhead than tearing apart and adding on to a 150 year old home in an historic district and converting it to a video arcade and photo processing studio.

Do-It-Yourselfers don't pay this percentage, but the cost they do pay is sometimes steep. Husbands become overwhelmed, cranky, and surly. There are times when they want to read the riot act to sub-contractors and tradesmen, but don't because they desperately want them to finish the job and get the heck out of their life. Also, these workers have the key to their house. The husband suffers stoically, then takes it out on his wife and family. Wives worry because the sweet guy they married has been sucked into a surreal landscape of plumbers joking among themselves about his family's excrement and non-English-speaking painters merrily applying the wrong color to the siding and oblivious to his protestations.

Do-It-Yourselfers beware: A project that is substantial enough to require the presence of sub-contractors and inspectors involves lots of planning, paperwork, and good organizational skills. Looking back, first timers will realize they remodeled their home through a trial and error process. Knowing what sub-contractors require in order to do their job, for example, takes lots of timing and communication. And don't forget, things will always come up that no one has thought of.

Contractors already know what kind of access a concrete truck needs to pour a foundation in the back yard, for example, and how much extra money and time is required if concrete needs to be pumped or wheeled. They check beforehand to see if full sheets of drywall can actually fit into the basement before they begin the project. They know how to fit a replacement tub into an old bathroom. Homeowners don't know where extra blocking for firestops, fixtures, and hardware is needed. Skilled contractors can look at a floor and know if it is too out of level to work around. Experience tells them when it is cost efficient and practical to tear up the floor and replace it. Rookie remodelers rarely make that call.

Do-It-Yourselfers who are determined to be their own general contractor because they believe they will pocket the contractor's fees should imagine for a moment that they will hire a top-notch firm to build their project. And then, ask themselves if this imaginary company would supply a superintendent with little building experience and a second job ("homeowner") to run the project? Would that be OK? Why not? Because the company knows it would lose money if the job were run by an inexperienced hand.

Guess what? Sub-contractors who bid a job with the knowledge that they will be working for an inexperienced homeowner may bump up their price because they fear the project will not be ready on schedule and the co-ordination among the trades that is essential will be lacking. And they may not feel like instructing the homeowner in the nuances, obvious or not, of bringing a job to completion.

Rookie D.I.Y.'ers who assume the General Contractor role on major projects can easily spend their projected savings on corrections because subcontractors were not adequately instructed, during the course of the job, about how to piece the project together. It takes experience to look at a blank subfloor and know how much room to allow in a short wall for a door, electrical boxes, trim, and heating registers.

Some rookie D.I.Y.'ers may not recognize substandard work, but are conned into paying for it anyway.

Remember, one thing that distinguishes the General Contractor and/or Field Superintendent from everyone else is that he/she alone is supposed to know all the answers and must function as the Central Brain on the job.

Sometimes, Mr. Homeowner gets consumed by the project and begins missing too much work from his real job, the one the bank is relying on him to keep to pay for this mess. Every morning, he spends two hours on the phone scheduling workers and imploring them to show up. He wastes endless hours waiting for sub-contractors and inspectors to arrive; trade professionals whose schedules are constantly skewed (through no fault of their own) by disasters on other projects. Unaccustomed to switching hats all day, from husband to contractor, the lines begin to blur. Eventually, Mr. Homeowner begins to treat Mrs. Homeowner like another laborer who didn't take out the trash. This is not a wise thing to do to a woman whose home resembles a natural disaster and is looking to her husband for answers.

She doesn't understand how beauty arises from chaos.

Like boxers in a ring, they square off and keep their distance from each other, only meeting to exchange jabs or drop the gloves to do something with the kids. If they are good sports and really love each other, they'll congratulate themselves at the end of the project. If not, the contractor's fees will seem cheap in hindsight, especially compared to a divorce lawyer.

In this Bizarro world, where major purchases like boats and cars are constructed on-site, imagine a new car being built in your dining room. For purposes of comparison, we know they cost about the same as a kitchen remodel.

Because of budget constraints, all you can afford is a Ford Taurus, a sensible family two-door. That new Lexus will just have to wait. You approve the model, the interior finish and options, weigh them against your budget, and the project begins.

The first thing you'll need is a port-a-potty in the front yard. It must be up front and accessible to the large truck that empties and cleans it every week. This precludes sticking it in the back, along the fence, or behind the bushes. Personally, I suggest placing it downwind from any windows.

A plastic outhouse will advertise to all of your neighbors you're about to spend lots of money – probably more than you'll know. If you're underway during the heat of July and August, the advertising will waft around the block. Roaming bands of teenagers out after curfew take delight in tipping over these unbalanced polyethylene closets. If the sight of a port-a-potty is too unsettling, you can always try to hide it next to the 30 yard dumpster that will be parked in the street. This dumpster will hold construction debris; left over trash from the worker's other jobs; and urine-stained mattresses, box springs, and old appliances your neighbors have been unable to get the regular trash service to haul off.

As the job progresses, these major lawn fixtures in your front yard will be complemented by smaller and more colorful signs that seemingly sprout up overnight. The architect and builder may have their own signs, and before long the siders and roofers and painters are bickering over your turf with their metal placards.

Your dining room furniture is now in the living room. The buffet is on the back porch. Narrow aisles among the tables and sofas allow for limited access. Plastic sheets are everywhere. A crew of carpenters has covered the dining room floor with a protective layer of plywood over the finished oak. Welders bring in the steel for your new car, assemble the frame, and as the axles, wheels, drive shaft and engine are added the thing begins to take shape. In a few days you are thrilled, despite the inconveniences.

Common sense says your car will take longer to construct in your home than on a production line. Henry Ford never became a titan of American industry because he went around building cars in each customer's garage, much less in the middle of the house. But this is what remodelers are required to do.

At the turn of the 20th century, American industry was comparatively backwards. Factory workers learned how jobs were performed from their foremen, fathers and relatives. This traditional approach was the industry standard until efficiency experts came on the scene after World War I. They measured and dissected and analyzed every movement and second of a worker's day, breaking every act of labor into the smallest detail, all to gain a fraction of a percentage in production and profit. The result? The Industrial Age shifts into overdrive.

Aside from remarkable advancements in tools, transportation, and communications, the remodeling industry's approach to construction has changed little in decades. No matter how much management spends on software programs and streamlines office procedures, inefficiency wants to rule in "The Field." Laborers sit on jobs and wait. Critical parts arrive sporadically. Someone accidentally sets off the house alarm, and the job sits for an hour until the police arrive to sort everything out. A carpenter can easily spend half a day plowing through traffic, hauling tools, setting up, actually working for thirty minutes, and then cleaning up to fix one piece of trim damaged by an anonymous worker.

Some of the workers who pass through your house may be idiots. Some may have criminal records. (An elderly woman in Grand Junction, Colorado, hired a handyman who swiped an urn from her mantel that contained her husband's ashes. The funeral urn was recovered some years later in Minnesota when the "handyman" was arrested after not returning 832 library books he had checked out. The man told investigators he took the urn in a dispute over money. A warrant had already been issued for him in Colorado on misdemeanor charges of abuse of a corpse and theft. When her late husband's ashes were finally returned, the 77 year-old widow said, "It's a little much.")

The workers in your home are following the trails and using the techniques they learned from their relatives and foremen, who learned how to "flash" a "cricket" from their dads and bosses. Sometimes, their business and accounting methods are just as antiquated.

Assembly line production and quality control; Old Man Ford might just as well toss them in that dumpster parked out front. The method of construction used in remodeling today would revert the automobile industry into a cottage industry.

Warning: Many of the workers on remodel jobs lack extensive training and instruction. Plumbers and electricians, for example, must pass standardized tests to operate legally, but they are the exception. In many jurisdictions, all a contractor needs for a license is cash and one certified employee on the payroll. Training is a critical investment in manpower many contractors are reluctant to make because of the the transitory nature of the work force. It doesn't make economic sense to pull someone off a paying job to attend safety and new product classes when that individual is going to leave town the next time a big hail storm hits Colorado or a tornado rakes Oklahoma. Or worse yet, leave the company to create their own business and compete against the company that trained them.

Homeowners may spot zombie-like workers prowling around the roof, armed with either a caulking gun or a paint brush that drips white splats on green shingles. These workers are distinguished by their inability to communicate or convey the essence of their daily task in any meaningful way. These workers are called "flat-liners" and "brain-stems." Their employment history can usually be traced to a blood relationship with a sub-contractor. I have seen "brain-stems" touch up exterior paint on the gable ends above a tile roof; their clod-hoppers punching holes in the fragile clay roof tiles, this destruction only a minor distraction to their task at hand. They are relatively easy to spot and should never be left unattended.

A majority of the workers in your home charge by the square foot. This is called, "piece work." Roofers, framers, drywallers, painters and floor guys all charge by the square foot, square yard, or just plain "square." This pricing system enables the general contractor bidding the work to predict costs with a fair level of accuracy and helps encourage competitive bidding among the "trades." Most of the workers on a large remodel get paid in this manner. Construction companies with a large payroll, in the home improvement field, are a rarity in the modern economic world. Taxes and other burdens escalate costs for hourly workers. Hourly wages don't always encourage timely completion. The downside to "piecework" is, this system often encourages workers to finish their jobs really fast because they're always in a hurry and if they don't rush rush rush and get on to the next job they won't make any money!

The general contractor (or homeowner) needs to review their work in great detail after they have finished and before they are paid.

Despite the historical influx of immigrants into the labor pool, it continues to shrink. The Bureau of Labor Statistics reports that the construction and home improvement fields will require approximately 240,000 new workers a year to meet current demands. Only 60,000 new workers are currently entering the field. Today's youth is seeking work in the high-tech fields, believing that market will provide them with the resources to buy new homes and cars. The trouble is, there is no one around to fix them.

Not long after the body of your Taurus is complete (the one in your dining room), you notice it's a bit too awkward to get into the back seat. Sure, you ordered a 2-door, but it turns out you really wanted a 4-door. You tell Mr. Ford you're really sorry, but it's important to get it the way we want it before the project gets too far along. You're aware of the added expense and delay, but feel it will be worthwhile. Mr. Ford agrees.

(*The might as well syndrome* has already kicked in. "As long as the house is torn up, we *might as well...*" fill in the blank. "Redo the deck, change the lights, repaint the house...")

The 4-door body goes on, and all is well. Mechanics get it running and in the middle of the night you're awake in bed realizing you should have put a bigger engine in too. You call Mr. Ford at 4 AM, at home, and he is none too happy to take your call, although he says he was up anyway to toss out the cat...

You ask him how much more another engine will cost.

A bigger engine won't bust the budget, but comes close. Mr. Ford will give you a full refund for the smaller engine, but of course you'll have to pay extra for removing the original, reinstalling a new one, and "Oh, by the way, the change order fee is 25%."

About all that's left now is paint and finish, and that begins while the new engine is trucked in. Painters mask and curtain off the entire house to ward against toxic fumes as the car is painted. But the color's not right. "It's not like the tiny chip the size of a postage stamp we liked so much in the design center." Turns out the color's exactly the same, but because the car's so much bigger and you're not under a fluorescent light anymore, the color just looks darker.

Mr. Ford is very clear: "This is exactly what you selected."

You repaint a lighter color. You pay for a lighter color.

Everyone is happy with the new color, especially the dog, who jumps up on the still tacky finish and smiles. The sympathetic painters repaint the rear quarter-panel for a small charge.

Now you've spent enough to have purchased that Lexus you really wanted in the first place.

Your wife has been keeping score the whole time, and this is a point she will constantly mention. Meanwhile, she's stressed out because her buffet is wrapped in plastic on the back porch, since there was no where else to store it. Some kind of rodent gnawed a hole in the back of the buffet, thinking it would make a nice place to live. Mr. Ford says the seats are on back order, which means the car will be done for a month by the time the seats arrive.

By the way, Mr. Ford needs to get paid most of the money for his car, now that it's substantially complete. It just needs two items – seats. Mr. Ford comes around once a month with his bill, just like clockwork, and he's due any day now.

This would make anyone crazy, yet this is the equivalent of what millions of Americans do every year. Remodeling is a multi-billion dollar industry. Home improvement's *annual* box office is equivalent to the Gross National Product of a couple of mid-sized European countries.

How much is that? In round numbers, around 185 billion dollars.

Homeowners in the United States believe their residences are falling apart and becoming hopelessly outdated at an alarming rate. Concerned citizens and professionals alike are doing all they can to stem this national crisis at any cost. Homeowners routinely spend more to renovate their homes than it would cost to replace them.

In retrospect, all homeowners conclude that their project took more of a toll on their time, bank accounts, and psyche than they expected. Additions, kitchens, and pop-tops become markers in a family's history like births, graduations, weddings, and deaths.

All projects can be equally frustrating for the novice or pro, from simply changing a switch (single or double pole, toggle or rocker, slide or touch, dimmer, lighted, white, ivory, almond, 3-way, 4-way, bipolar or manic depressive) to gutting a house (and finding the estimated costs double).

The process of remodeling is about solving problems. The first rule is to keep little problems from turning into big problems, or else Remodeling Dementia may set in.

I have been a serial remodeler for thirty years and have been reading home-improvement books for just as long. The information they present can be valuable, but that information needs to be honed by experience to be effective.

The single key to completing a job on-time and on-budget is to anticipate and sidestep problems on a daily basis.

It is simple math to conclude that a homeowner or contractor who has to redo their work will take longer to reach the finish line and not be cost-effective.

This is not a comprehensive reference manual. This is the guidebook of on-the-job problems. Aside from "Mississippi Man's" experience, the following pages contain tales of scheduling, seduction, allowances, death, change orders, and criminal behavior. If you learn anything, it will be to keep problems in their place, where they belong, and to find them before they find you.

You are not reading a "how-to" book. This is a "how-not-to" book, based on the notion we all learn from our mistakes, for goof-ups always seem to create a more indelible impression than the tiny triumphs that make up a day.

2 GOLDILOCKS

Who *is* that passed out on my bed?

First impressions are crucial, especially when I'm the following act for every homeowner's worst nightmare.

Marsha R___ invited me into her condo in a very exclusive section of town. My partner and I had contracted to do the warranty work for the entire block of town homes. They were just a year old, and most of the problems weren't too serious.

The biggest single disaster was Wendy G___'s, on the corner. The P-trap in her large whirlpool tub was located too close to an outside wall, not insulated, and a sub-zero draft during the first winter caused it to freeze and burst. As she drained the bath water that frigid morning, the joist cavities above her dining room filled with water. After dressing she went downstairs to witness three hundred gallons of water raining onto her dining room set. Water gushed through the chandelier; the drywall sagged, and melon-sized blisters of bath water developed in the paint. Silk curtains and upholstery, an inlaid table – all ruined. The G___'s was the talk of the block until Marsha R___'s hit the top of the list.

Marsha was an attractive, well-dressed, and successful business-woman. Her name was familiar because it adorned several car dealer-ships. We got along great. I had done lots of warranty work in the past, and was sensitive to the homeowner's wishes whenever I was working in their home. The banker on this project was a longtime associate, and he basically just dropped the job in our laps. Soon I was to know why.

The punch list consisted of adjusting some doors, miscellaneous

11

caulking and grouting, and replacing a defective light fixture. Easy stuff. We walked through her home, reviewed the items on the list, and then she confided to me about the last "warranty guy."

Marsha came home for lunch that first day to see if he needed any help or had any questions. She gave him free reign over the house. He seemed like a nice guy, she said. The builder was reliable and she trusted him to send out qualified workers. Marsha knew he was inside that day because his truck was still parked on the street, and she hollered up the stairwell to announce her presence – she didn't want to startle him.

She needn't have worried.

It seems he had gotten into several "X-rated" video tapes she told me "her ex-husband had left in the back of the closet, on the top shelf. What he was doing up there, I have no idea."

Evidently he perused the selections, saw the wide screen TV and VCR opposite the foot of the bed and, in a perverse sort of way, added 2 plus 2.

His lack of judgment was further compounded by the fact that he had gotten into her good scotch at some point in the morning, and imbibed just enough to pass out about a half hour before the lady of the house arrived home.

And there she found him, just like Goldilocks, only snoring on her bed and oblivious to the shenanigans now on the TV.

Marsha turned off the tube, called her next door neighbor, and the two of them roused him from his stupor and hustled him out of the house to sleep it off in his truck.

I later asked Walt L___, the banker, about this story, and he laughed heartily as he confirmed it. I was relieved that it really happened and wasn't a fairy tale Marsha told everyone who worked in her home.

P.S. A few weeks later our company got a nice thank-you note from Marsha, commending my professionalism, workmanship, and courtesy. We framed it and hung it on the wall, where it fit just right.

3 CONTRACTORS FROM HELL

Homeowners are terrified one will walk onto their property, legitimate contractors wish they would go away and stop ruining their good reputations, the law rarely catches and prosecutes them, and they go through the world like the disgusting, foul, evil, primordial demons from Hell that they are. In their wake are wrecked homes, unpaid bills, and countless hours and days wasted in their pursuit. They are sick. Their behavior is a pattern of abuse. They are criminals.

GRAND AWARD SLEAZY CONTRACTORS WHO TAKE A BIG DOWN PAYMENT, THEN SKIP. They may tear off *some* of your roof or dig out just the hole in your yard, then disappear. Usually your money has financed a bad personal habit or robbed Peter to pay Paul. Often they work a few days, then pull off the job for a seemingly legitimate excuse. But as their absence becomes more and more worrisome, the excuses tend to get flimsier and flimsier. Before long, they stop returning your calls or acknowledging your existence. This category snares the top spot because of prevalence, money lost, and degree of aggravation. Other individual cases in different categories may prove more heinous, but the entrants in this category are the ones who annually propel contractors to the top of the Better Business Bureau's complaint list.

A stucco contractor screwed me once. This particular project was started by a previous homeowner, and purchased as a distressed property/fixer-upper (I'm being kind here) by the homeowner who hired me. Bill S___ was young and willing to put in plenty of sweat-equity, but he needed someone to take on a challenge in the home-improvement arena.

13

That was me.

The previous owner was a wild-eyed maniac. I knew this because the house was only a few blocks away from my own. In fact, I often walked past it on summer evenings with my family, usually during an after-dinner stroll to 7-11 for ice cream. He was gaunt, had a full beard, and was often heard yelling and screaming in the house. No doubt things were getting to him. I recognized him from one of the lumberyards; the neighborhood scuttlebutt, as filtered through the kids, was that he was an abusive man.

He left the place a disaster. It was a rectangular stucco ranch with two bedrooms partially added in the back. The kitchen cabinets were new, but they didn't match each other. It appeared as though he collected returns from the lumber yard, scratched and dinged stuff, and put them together like a jig-saw puzzle. The result was a jumbled blend of styles - Cathedral and Modern – and colors – cherry and oak. The roof was half torn off – there were gaping holes all around the building. The permit situation with the city was a mess. There had been no inspection for over a year. One evening I remember seeing him shovel partially set-up concrete out of the back of his pick-up into forms he built to create a sidewalk. When it set up (which was before he emptied his truck), the end product more closely resembled the frosting a four-year old might have applied to her first bakery effort.

My agreement with Bill S___ was to do all required repairs to get the

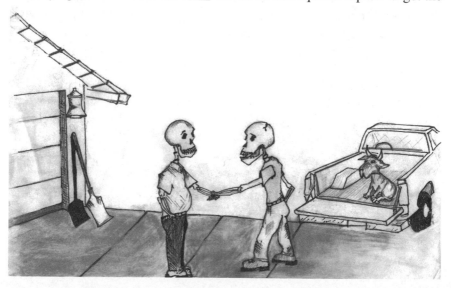

roof and gutter on, sub out roofing and gutters, repair or rebuild sheathing as needed, get the place stuccoed, get the permits in order, and change a few doors and windows while we were at it. Bill tackled things like jack hammering concrete from the front of the house and laying fresh sod.

Over a dozen stucco contractors looked at the place. It was obvious no one wanted to touch the project, and who could blame them? Celotex panels flapped wildly at the top of the parapet, the framing was a joke, and all the existing construction details were wrong. So when Ron B___ agreed to stucco the house, I was more than happy to give him a $1200 down payment (about one third) to begin the project.

He worked three short days before he stopped showing up and I was on his butt. Over the next month I heard every excuse in the book.

Ron B___ was a beer-bellied ex-Marine in his early sixties, adept at promising the world and then peeing all over it. At the end of the fourth day, after not showing up at all, I drove to his home and banged on his door around 6:00 PM. He answered the door in his pajamas, said he just got in from Wyoming, (which seemed strange at the time) but promised to be on the job at 9:00 AM the next morning.

No Ron B___ the next morning, but his laborer was on the job, waiting. And waiting. His story was, he only worked for him a few days, had his own concerns about getting paid, and left after a few hours. Ron, we were told, "was on his way."

He never showed up that day; he wasn't home that night. He must have been out walking his pet rat.

Then, he couldn't find a laborer, had high blood pressure, couldn't get the right medication, worked half a day a week, promised to be done in two weeks and, due to my persistent questioning, eventually came up with the all-time best excuse.

The Pope was in town that week for World Youth Day, an international event. About three weeks into this fiasco, he told me he *"had to go visit the Pope."*

Because he showed up every now and then, this case was a civil matter, not a criminal matter. Had he just taken the check and disappeared, the police would have considered him a thief. But slime-balls like Ron B___ know police in a big city have better things to do than track them down. The only exception is when a district attorney has evidence of a pattern of fraud and/or preying on the elderly.

The only recourse a citizen has is to sue in civil court. I won my suit against Ron B___ for everything I asked for. But, after reviewing his file

15

at the DA's office, so did a lot of other people. Ron B___ made sure he didn't have a pot to piss in, so no one could collect any damages against him. All of his assets were in his wife's name.

I did, however, keep his scaffolding, cement mixer, and other miscellaneous tools. He did admit his debt and allowed me to keep them. They weren't worth much to me but at least I had the satisfaction of keeping him out of business. Vociferous complaints at the classified section of both major newspapers caused them to pull his ads, keeping him unemployed.

I eventually found a great guy who finished the job for not much more than what we had left in the budget. I landed on my feet dollars and cents-wise, but thinking of Ron B___ is bad for my blood pressure.

The lesson, of course, is to pay as you go or pay for materials as they are delivered. Payment terms need to be spelled out clearly before the job begins. This won't eliminate future problems (Ron B___'s contract was very clear) but may help.

Homeowners need to thoroughly investigate contractors who require large down payments. Longstanding businesses have accounts with suppliers for pick-up and delivery of materials. Contractors who may be in financial difficulty no longer have accounts with suppliers. Giving large amounts of cash to these creatures is foolhardy.

To hire a Contractor from Hell, select a company that has not been in business for very long under the same name; hire a company that doesn't have licenses in many jurisdictions; Contractors from Hell probably aren't members of any industry trade associations, certainly aren't members of the Better Business Bureau, and don't have any suppliers or bankers as references.

Small "Mom and Pop" shops may not meet all of these qualifications; some independent sub-contractors may not either, for a number of reasons. Tradesmen who run their own businesses are an independent lot. Skilled and reliable craftsmen often shy away from affiliating themselves with trade organizations. Plus, they may be a homeowner's best bet for a small job. The bottom line is to check references, ask questions, and employ some intuition.

Some bad contractors go belly up about as often as a snake sheds its skin. When this happens, they leave a trail of bad debts and unfinished work. By reincorporating under a similar but different name, they avoid responsibility and attempt to dodge creditors. "S&M Construction" can become "S&M Remodeling" and continue their shady practices under a different name.

Many firms that specialize in custom products, like cabinets, counter tops, custom millwork and blinds, legitimately collect down payments because otherwise they might be left with a finished product and a homeowner who has changed his or her mind.

In a perfect world, major projects that take a few months to complete generally work this way: S&M Construction presents the homeowner with bills for the month at the end of the month. The bills are from the subs and suppliers for concrete, lumber, labor, engineering, anything and everything that went into the job during the prior 30 days. There may even be a "down payment" for the cabinets in the first bill. The contractor lists all of these expenses in his bill to the homeowner. He may even charge for items that have been delivered to the job site, but the contractor has not yet been billed for. He will figure in his own time as is appropriate. The contractor is usually under no obligation to show the homeowner his copy of the bill, because it may not reflect his markup on certain items. (More about markups later).

S&M's bill is reviewed by the architect, (if there is one) who confirms that what was billed for was delivered and the work was satisfactorily completed. This is especially helpful for homeowners who are inexperienced with construction. The architect, in most cases, is an advocate for the homeowner and is paid by the homeowner. In a perfect world, the architect approves payment to S&M Construction, and the homeowner cuts the check. If applicable, the bank managing the construction funds gets the bill, the letter from the architect or owner, and cuts the check. If there is a dispute of some kind over one or two items, the check gets cut less the disputed amount. Then, the dispute is resolved among the concerned parties ASAP so a second check can be cut.

In this perfect world, S&M Construction pays its suppliers and subcontractors 30 days after their bill is received. Subcontractors will work one month, knowing they won't get paid 'till next month, because S&M Construction has a history of paying its bills on time. The entire process, from the time the homeowner receives the bill until the contractor gets a check, may take about week.

It's very simple. The contractor presents the bill around the end of the month, the contractor gets a check around the beginning of the month, and the subs and suppliers get their checks after the 10th or so. Homeowners who are intent on being a fly in the ointment go directly to the "Homeowners From Hell" chapter.

There are several variations on this payment scenario; it is offered only as a general guideline. Homeowners may pay directly for materials, or they may pay subs directly, DEPENDING ON WHAT IS SPELLED OUT IN THE CONTRACT.

Smaller jobs are often handled by a single individual. In a case like this, it is very appropriate to "pay as you go," usually weekly. Pay bills for materials as they come in, or when the product is delivered. Pay for labor at the end of the job or the end of the week, whatever comes first.

The only defense consumers have against getting ripped off is to get educated about these vermin.

FIRST PLACE SHODDY WORKMANSHIP. Doors that don't close, roofs that leak, additions that sink, and big-gapped trim are all evidence of shoddy workmanship.

Reputable contractors return to fix mistakes. Bad contractors may deny a problem exists, discredit the homeowner, and then ask the homeowner to "be specific" about "what exactly is wrong" *ad nauseum*. They may apologize. If the money involved is not significant, they may not come back.

But where is the bar that distinguishes "shoddy workmanship" from the old saw that has been a fixture in construction contracts for years – "... done in a workmanlike manner."?

There are no clear-cut answers.

Homes are constructed to certain minimum standards. The UBC (Universal Building Code) outlines minimum standards of construction, and these are enforced (with local modifications) by the building department. The inspector makes sure a project is wired and plumbed according to national standards, that shingles are installed according to manufacturer's recommendations, and that window glazing is appropriate for the intended use. This is to ensure public safety; that buildings don't collapse, citizens aren't electrocuted, potable water is not cross-contaminated, etc. A residence must meet certain structural requirements, and these are routinely checked by the local building department. Interior fit and finish, while understandably a big issue to a paying customer, is of little consequence to a building inspector.

Should a project flunk these *minimum* standards, as outlined by local authorities, the contractor should not be paid until the problem is corrected. (Important note: Most major projects have a few glitches with the building department. Remodeling is especially complicated because old and new don't always fit. Reputable builders, while looking out for their client's best interests, also co-operate with the building department. Routine corrections are usually considered a part of the job--miscellaneous blocking and additional nailing or strapping are rarely causes for alarm.) If a sub-contractor is at fault, and has already been paid, the general contractor will often withhold future payments until the required corrections are made.

This is why periodic and scheduled inspections are so critical. If the project is not within the scope of the building department, a mutually agreed upon third party may be helpful as the job progresses. Tackle problems as they develop. If they are ignored, they will only get bigger. A homeowner's main recourse is financial – withholding payment. Best advice – deal with problems before they get too big to ignore. (See "Problems" chapter).

In the real world, most projects are completed according to minimum standards without too much difficulty. Homeowners who complain about shoddy workmanship are usually thinking of the drywall joints that show only after their home lighting is turned on and their furniture is in. Doors that warp at the top or suck cold air come to mind. Big caulk joints point out sloppy work like a neon finger. If the carpenter didn't bring his two best friends, Level and Plumb, to the job then all Hell can break loose. In fairness, Level and Plumb should already be there. If not, the marriage of old and new will be a bad fit.

Smart contractors will "square up" a room or roof during the estimating process. Smart contractors will point out the absence of their best friends before work begins, and price accordingly. Square tiles on an out-of-level floor, especially contrasting colors, only highlight a problem. Smart contractors and homeowners know this.

The "level of finish" is what distinguishes superb contractors from run of the mill contractors and Contractors from Hell. The difference in the level of workmanship between an expensive custom home and a tract home, for example, should be a world apart. Trim joints should be perfect in a custom. In tract work, perfect is not mandatory.

Margins around a door, for example, can vary by one-sixteenth, one-eighth, or one-quarter inch. This gap between the door and frame, however, should be consistent. A group of ten carpenters, contractors, and millwork suppliers judging one simple door may not reach agreement on the quality of finish unless the door installation was perfect or terrible. Old timers suggest this gap should equal the thickness of a nickel, thus giving the homeowners their "nickel's worth."

In a quality job, that door at the end of the hallway will be centered on the wall with even margins of casing and wall around the frame. The reveal of the trim will be consistent. So too will the margins.

If the project is a window replacement, remember it's easy to install a leaky window that is not properly flashed. Replacing or finishing broken sills and trim distinguishes a craftsman from someone blowing through your home who is not making enough money on the job to go back and fix all the little things.

The best guideline in a remodel is that the workmanship should match or be consistent with the original house. Homeowners who expect a higher standard than "existing" should point out existing problems or tacky work during the bid process. Contractors should build to the rest of the house, be it a palace or a slum.

The National Association of Home Builders publishes a manual titled, *Residential Construction Performance Guidelines*. It is updated every few years, and is designed to resolve disputes between builders and homeowners before they wind up in court. Ever wondered when brush strokes on an interior painted surface are too visible? Now you can look it up!

Contractors from Hell claiming First Prize don't build to minimum standards, leave work that is sub-standard compared to the original, and don't bother or aren't capable of fixing their messes.

SECOND PLACE FLY-BY NIGHT ARTISTS. They roam from city to city like itinerant gypsies, loosely-knit families like the Mob, taking advantage of elderly and unsuspecting homeowners. They promise something that is too good to be true. Guess what? It is! They spray driveways and roofs with over-priced sealers. They call after the first chill of fall and say they are running a "special" in your neighborhood, and will check your furnace for half price! Such a deal! They are RIP-OFF AND SCAM ARTISTS who charge thousands for work that isn't needed.

Like vampires, they can't pass through your door unless they're invited. They'll change your furnace filter, lube the motor, and then terrify the homeowner by telling them their "heat exchanger is cracked. If you run this thing, carbon monoxide will fill your house and kill you all in the middle of the night. You'll need a whole new furnace. The good news is I can get you one today for only (the entire balance of your checking account.)" Or, "The gas line has a bad valve. Good thing you called us."

Right. They threaten your lives to make a buck. They may as well wear black hoods and break into your home in the middle of the night.

The truth is, heat exchangers rarely crack. They are not a maintenance item like a clogged gutter or faucet washers. The heat exchanger is a metal box that collects the heated air the furnace generates. It is very difficult to see inside the box, which precludes a homeowner from making their own inspection. (Legitimate firms use a tester that diagnoses a defective box.) The box usually has some rust because of ambient moisture in the air that creates oxidizion on the interior walls, but this alone does not mean the part is defective. Homeowners typically feel at the mercy of the man in the blue coveralls with the little flashlight when they are coaxed into making a decision about a major financial expenditure. And the words, "GAS LEAK" create visions of a home exploding in the middle of the night, the occupants' bodies flying into the trees.

These are, of course, real hazards. But the best way to avoid a "misdiagnosis" is to spend a little extra to hire an established firm to annually inspect and service the home heating system. If they suggest expensive repairs, get a second opinion. Ask them to quantify or show you what the problem is. Electronic sniffers can measure carbon monoxide and gas leaks.

A reputable firm will do the following:

Change the filter.

Clean the heat exchanger and check the integrity of the unit.

Clean and lube the air-handler fan.

Check both air and fuel flow.

Test the draft pressure.

Check for carbon monoxide.

Check all controls and adjust if needed.

Remember: Call a good firm before a bad one comes calling on you!

THIRD PLACE CONTRACTORS WHO SCREW CONSUMERS ON CARPETING. It usually happens on the tail end of a job, when a lot of bills pile in and things get a little crazy. There are a few ways to take it in the rear, so here's what to look for:

Double-check all measurements. Carpeting is sold by the yard. A yard of carpet is a piece that measures 3'x 3' – 9 sq. ft. In simple figures, a 12'x 12' room (144 sq. ft.) is 16 yards (144 divided by 9 equals 16.)

Carpet layers will need to account for waste and proper seaming in their figures. If there is a pattern, the waste percentage will climb higher. Wise homeowners are clear on how much carpet is figured, how much is ordered, and how much it costs. They will also check waste at the end of a job. Unscrupulous carpet-layers can pad their figures by 15% to 20%.

Study the padding that goes under the carpet. There are two things to look for: Thickness and density. Most padding is one-half inch, and thicker padding (three-quarters) does not necessarily mean better. In most cases, the carpet manufacturer will recommend the proper matching thickness.

Carpeting can last longer if homeowners upgrade the "weight" of their padding at a small cost. Good padding can make less expensive carpeting feel and perform better. A six or eight pound "weight" is a good density. Contractors from Hell may supply padding so lightweight, and cheap, that the entire project may seem ruined.

Dumb consumers will be led around by the nose in their carpet selections, chasing the cheapest deal around. Again, a reputable firm may charge a fraction more for their product, but that is very cheap insurance against getting ripped off. Wise homeowners want a reputable firm that will stand behind its work and correct minor glitches in the installation.

When carpet layers finish a job, it's not their responsibility to vacuum the house. Picking up trash and hauling off scraps is the extent of their obligation. After vacuuming, "whiskers" pop up and seams may not completely lay down. There may be "bumps" along the edges, by the walls, and the carpet may need to be kicked around a little bit. Reputable firms have a crew that specifically attends to these details. Contractors from Hell have a pager or fax number that consumers call and no one answers. Ever.

Carpet layers have to remove doors prior to installation. At the end of the job, they rehang them. If door bottoms don't clear the new carpeting, it's not the carpet-layer's job to trim doors. On a large project, the job superintendent or general contractor knows this and has them installed at the correct height in the first place or arranges to trim the doors after the carpet-layers have left. Homeowners responsible for their own installation should ask the salesperson about these details when the job is being measured, and line up a carpenter to follow the carpet-layers. These same homeowners need to call the painter back, because baseboard is often scuffed and scraped during installation.

Bad carpeting can ruin a job, so it is incumbent upon the homeowner to beware of the pitfalls. The carpet sample in the showroom may not match the product trucked in from Georgia. An "upgrade" may only be a fabric protector. Homeowners strapped for cash at the end of the job try to save money contracting their own carpeting and can sometimes lose sight of who they are dealing with.

While carpet yardage is an easy way to get screwed by Contractors from Hell, wise homeowners will double-check all measurements – tile, paint, flooring, stucco – of contractors that charge by area. If the numbers don't seem to add up, simply ask the contractor to explain the figures. There is probably a logical explanation. If the explanation does not seem logical, ask a trustworthy tradesperson for a second opinion before assuming the worst.

Susan H___ bought new carpet for the old home she was moving into. She stopped by the house after work the day the carpet layers finished, only to realize they had installed the wrong product! It was close, but clearly not what she ordered. According to the terms of the contract she signed at the showroom, she was to pay for the installation of so many yards of ABC carpet. Instead, she got XYZ carpet. Susan wanted to hold them to the contract, but the job was already done. Legally, Susan could have made them tear out XYZ and replace it with ABC. But they compromised: Susan paid for padding and installation, and got the wrong carpet for free.

Homeowners want the contractors and tradesmen who work in their homes to meet certain minimal criteria. Homeowners think contractors should be competent and do a good job. They should be communicative, especially about problems (See "Problems" chapter) and delays. It's always important to interview contractors beforehand and ask questions. Ask about the crews that will work in your home. Do they speak English if there is a problem? If not, who can we call?

Would you be concerned if the crew acted like panelists from the "Jerry Springer Show"? If not, why?

If your project is time-consuming and expensive, it's not out of line to meet or observe crew members on other jobs. Ask the contractor to make the necessary arrangements.

When homeowners hire an unfamiliar contractor to work on their home the Big Fear is they will be cheated and screwed out of money.

People who operate out of fear, of course, are more likely to make bad choices than sensible choices. The contractor with the highest bid may have included all possible contingencies in his estimate. Homeowners don't realize they are more likely to get screwed by a Contractor from Hell who underbids and can't finish the project or finishes it cheaply and badly. In almost all instances, backtracking and repairs will cost more in dollars and aggravation than paying top dollar in the first place.

Homeowners need to judge before they hire someone, *Will they get the value for their dollar they expect?*

To the astonishment of many contractors, discriminating homeowners will look for many qualities in the crew that shows up at the door. Aside from a good job at a fair price, homeowners hope to find integrity, confidence, and honesty. Some homeowners are relieved to be greeted with workers who exhibit good grooming and personal hygiene.

You will not only be working with these people, you'll be living with them. And the last place you'll want to live together is Hell.

4 DID YOU KNOW?

An upside down electrical plug indicates a switched outlet.

Finish nails should be set to a depth equal to the width of the head.

It's possible to sell or donate (for a nice tax break) small to medium sized trees slated for removal. Check with nurseries or the local Parks and Recreation Department. Homeowners can donate used cabinets, windows, doors and other house parts in good condition to Habitat For Humanity. The organization warehouses donated building materials and incorporates them into

housing for first-time homeowners. Remember, the biggest thing you can recycle is your house!

A house between 10 and 20 years old is usually the biggest candidate for repairs. Roofing, water heaters, carpeting and furnaces are some of the big-ticket items whose life expectancy ends by then. A study sponsored by the *Wall Street Journal* concluded homeowners can expect to spend 4 times the purchase price, over 30 years, to keep a house maintained in very good condition.

Concrete trucks are regarded as the heaviest vehicles on the road. These *driveway busters*, when topped off, can weigh in at 70,000 pounds.

Trim and millwork suppliers will not warranty a wood door that is eight feet tall against warpage.

The National Association of Home Builders believes these home features, if properly installed, will last at least 100 years; copper wiring, a brick or stone wall, and slate shingles.

Pressure-treated lumber is easily recognized by its pale green tint. It is designed for below grade structural applications and is commonly used in decks and playground equipment. The material is treated with CCA (copper chromated arsenic), which is poisonous, toxic, and a known carcinogen. Burning scraps and inhaling the sawdust can cause sickness. CCA is banned in some countries and states. The EPA has asked retailers to voluntarily post warnings in the marketplace in lieu of stricter regulations. These warnings often appear as yellow tags about the size of a return address label stapled onto the ends of the planks: Chromated Copper Arsenate (CCA-C) Notice: Ask Dealer For A Copy of the Warranty and Consumer Information and Handling Guide (Text reprinted actual size.)

Many concrete contractors won't warranty concrete flatwork against spalling or flaking unless it is sealed annually with a high-priced sealer.

Contractors generally charge more (15-20%) if the client is a female, based on the notion she will change her mind, thus causing job delays and cost overruns.

Contractors in many states have a legal obligation to notify homeowners if they uncover asbestos during the course of an inspection or remodel.

The chances of a homeowner, as opposed to an asbestos worker, contracting asbestosis from a casual exposure, according to doctors and experts, is "extremely remote" or "practically zero." These phrases imply odds of 1 in 10,000 or 1 in 1,000,000.

Black & Decker marketed the first electric pistol grip drill in 1916. Skil introduced the first portable circular saw in 1924. For remodelers, Milwaukee unveiled the first portable reciprocating saw in 1951.

In 2002, Black & Decker marketed a retro design electric drill for nostalgia buffs.

The Environmental Protection Agency (EPA) requires all remodelers who perform work on housing constructed before 1978 provide residents with a copy of their pamphlet, "Protect Your Family From Lead in Your Home." All remodelers must keep a signed disclosure statement from the residents in their files for three years. Minor work that affects less than two square feet is exempt. Penalties of up to $25,000 a day may be issued to violators.

Phillips screws provide the style of head tradesmen prefer. Their distinctive cross-shaped head is widely preferred over the traditional straight-slotted screw head.

Manufacturers in the 1920's were searching for a better design for production work, as traditional heads were wildly inefficient and unable to withstand the rigors of mass-production assembly lines.

Enter Oregon inventor J.P. Thompson. He shopped his patented design for a self-centering and vibration-resistant screw to several screw manufacturers who liked his idea but concluded that it was impossible to manufacture because stamping the cross would destroy the head.

A dejected Thompson sold the rights to an acquaintance who shopped it around some more until eventually scoring with American Screw. The man convinced Eugene Clark, American Screw's president, that production of the improved design was possible with a few modifications. Mr. Clark, keenly aware that all industries were eager for this new product, put his considerable resources behind the project and began selling Henry

Phillips' improved design to industry by 1936.

General Motors first put them to use in 1937 Cadillacs. By 1940, 85% of the screw industry came on board. In a couple of years, they became an indispensable part of the war effort.

Although he retired in 1945 and passed away thirteen years later, the Phillips Screw Company that Henry Phillips founded in 1934 still exists today.

Some major plumbing firms that specialize in service calls actually instruct their plumbers to hem and haw, scratch their heads, and propose extensive and unnecessary repairs to homeowners.

To many other plumbers, no instruction is necessary.

In construction worker parlance, a clusterfuck is:

a. A convergence of poorly designed and ill-fitting walls, corners, trim, tile, wiring, piping, and/or finish materials.

b. Several tradesmen on a large project having to simultaneously work in an area of 100 square feet or less.

c. Two or more bureaucrats on a single job site.

d. All of the above.

5
HERCULES AND THE FLYING BREASTS

Hercules could have been a movie star. He was Jaws, Cujo, and Godzilla packed into 200 lbs. of brindled fur. Snarling, snapping, drooling, roaring – frantically charging against and digging under a chain link fence with one intent – to take a piece out of my kiester.

Hercules was the biggest pit bull I had ever seen. The thought of me going into *his* house, working in *his* basement, and walking on *his* floor drove the big lout totally bonkers. The rattle of my engine and my truck door slamming shut incited the beast on a daily basis, and by the time I knocked on the front door every morning he was foaming at the mouth from his bone crusher mandibles. While I never took any satisfaction from tormenting him by my sheer presence, I did make a point of taking a snapshot of him one day because he was so...huge. And ferocious. I think the camera flash set him off, like King Kong, and the chances of us ever making peace dropped from slim to none.

Terry and Marie A___ lived in a green house with a brown lawn. It was a dinge joint if I ever saw one. The backyard looked out over a large dry wash that turned into runway number three at the International Airport. Every fifteen minutes the house rattled like a cheap coupe tearing down a washboard road. One day I was working on the patio cover when a jet flew so low I could see faces peering out the window, wondering where in the Hell it was they were about to land. I waved up, and someone flying in from Chicago pointed me out. I finished a couple of basement rooms for them and built a patio cover. They weren't great clients, but Terry had a knack for calling when things were slow.

29

Hercules' owners insisted he was very nice, but was "protective" of his immediate family. His "Mommy" was a buxom platinum blonde from Belgium, a nurse at the local Army hospital. She claimed she was a hoofer when she was young, but by the time I met her she was neither. His "Daddy" was semi-retired from the military and spent his evenings stoned on booze and chain-smoking in his basement. Terry had a sad-faced mug, chalky white behind big thick-rimmed glasses. To know what his expression was like, look in the mirror and pull the outsides of your eyes toward your ears, then look up.

Terry and Marie lived in two different worlds. He worked days and spent nights in the basement. She worked swing shift and lived upstairs. If they left notes for each other, they were being communicative. Not exactly lovebirds.

The basement was always cool and dark, just like a cave. The smell of Chesterfields and old cigar butts hung in the air. By 4:30 every afternoon I could usually find him down there guzzling a bottle of hooch. After his first DUI his mouthpiece kept him out of the icebox by promising the judge Terry would keep his nose clean. After he got pinched for his second DUI the fine doubled and Terry was sentenced to community service. He handed me a cheap can crusher one afternoon, and in his gurgly voice asked me if I could put it up on the wall someplace. With a poker face, he told me his community service was recycling aluminum, and he came home with a case of Bud to get the show on the road. I never questioned him about it; Terry wasn't much for snappy patter in the first place, so I screwed the damn thing on the wall while he cracked open a case of beer.

Marie was in a much better humor most of the time. She usually got up around 9:00 AM to let me in and stayed in the bedroom or lounged on the divan. Sometimes she baked Belgian pastries in the kitchen or cooked up a great smelling dish for lunch or to leave for Terry when he got home. Cooking was something she really enjoyed, and she often broke into song as she hustled about in her kitchen. She spoke with a lilting Belgian accent through some really crooked teeth. I couldn't quite tell if the lisp was from her teeth or her nation of origin, but suspected the former.

Marie liked to play with her two budgies. On really cold days she set them by an open door insisting the cold fresh air was good for them. It sure made them perkier, but I was skeptical. I figured it was just a practice from the Old Country. All I knew was my wife would die if any of her budgies got near a draft on a cold day.

I think she was kind of sweet on me, but number one, I'm a married man; number two, it's bad business to mess with a client.

One day the inevitable happened. I returned from lunch and knocked on the door. Marie was getting dressed for work and answered the door in her robe to let me in, then went back to the bedroom to finish dressing. All the while I can hear Hercules snapping and howling in the other bedroom, working himself into a fit. I was packing some tools, so I went around to the back door to bring them down into the basement instead of walking through the front room. It was cold outside so I shut the back door as I walked through the kitchen and began the long walk to the basement door.

Suddenly, the bedroom door splintered and I could hear Hercules' charging roar echo through the hall. I would never make either door in time, so I drew my hammer from my belt loop and cocked my arm. I put a death grip on a 28 oz. Vaughn framing hammer with a waffle face and a 16" hickory handle. It was no Smith and Wesson, but it would have to do. I figured I would nail him as soon as he leaped for my throat. Right between the eyes. Bury that sucker in the top of his skull.

It's almost spooky how things happen in a life and death situation. On the one hand, everything happens in a split-second. That's in real time. My thinking was very clear yet, oddly enough, everything seemed to be going in slow motion too. Right behind Hercules ran a screaming Marie, dressed only in her panties. The bosomy Belgian was screaming, "NOOO-OO-O!!!" and reaching for his collar. Mindless of everything else, her breasts were swinging wildly in all directions at once. For a nanosecond I realized what kind of dancing she might have done in her youth while this slow motion fiasco unfolded...

But this was not exactly a day with Bo Derek at the beach. Hercules' fetid breath snapped me back to reality as Marie collared him at the last second, then covered herself up with one arm as best she could. My hammer may have been cocked, but my face was white. I think he lost some traction on the slick vinyl when he hit the kitchen, and that proved to be the difference between life and death. Whose life and death, I'm still not sure. She scolded the brute in French all the way back to her own bedroom, the one with a good lock, and apologized up and down after she made herself decent.

Too bad there's never a camera around when you need one.

Psychotic Remodeling

6
THIS HOUSE STINKS

Wally S___ was a plumbing contractor on a new subdivision of tract homes. The builder offered a few different styles, and they could be customized to a certain extent during construction to suit the new owner's taste and budget. Windows and doors could be moved or enlarged, and basements could be finished or even deleted.

One particular residence was just underway when the new owners decided to eliminate their basement and convert it to a crawl space. Floor framing had just begun and the basement drains had been "roughed-in." Since the concrete floor had not been poured, Wally S___stubbed a 4 inch drain pipe to the top of the foundation wall to tie into later. The framing crew pulled off for a day, and the basement was filled with another five feet of soil by a backhoe, graded by hand, and then the sub-floor, etc., was finished.

A couple of weeks later Wally S___ returned to finish his regularly scheduled "rough-in" and tied everything together under the house; the new buyers moved in on time some months later, and all was happy and bright in their new world.

The D___ family went about their daily business – a family of four will typically run over ten thousand gallons of water down the drain in a month's time. Dishwashers, washing machines, bathrooms, and what goes down the proverbial kitchen sink seemed to run non-stop in their busy household. The D___'s toilets alone consumed 4.5 gallons per flush.

But about six months later the edges of their bright world in their shiny new home began to darken and stain. A malodorous spectre – the scent of rotting trash, backed up urinals, and dead organisms began to per-meate their house. At first they thought maybe a cat had left a bird or mouse to decompose in an inaccessible area, or one of the little kids had some kind of bodily function misfire in a corner of the house and failed to report it.

The odor never left, only intensified, and after a week or two of phone tag and conversations between the now-concerned owners and the builder, Wally S___ finally arrived to investigate.

The owners made a short story long, telling Wally S___ in great detail how they first noticed the smell, what they thought it might be, and soon Wally's heart sank. "Oh, shit," he thought. In his heart he knew this was not going to be a simple backed up pipe or clogged vent.

The owners followed him into the laundry room and handed him a flashlight as he opened the access door to the crawl space. An overpowering stench of a well-known substance that usually rolled down hill knocked everyone over. Raw sewage was floating within a foot of the floor framing, indicating the crap was over two feet deep in their crawl space. Spread out over a 1600 square foot area, that calculates to about 23,680 gallons of raw sewage. Enough, in other words, to make everyone sick.

Wally began to pump it out that day, and for the rest of the week two pumps ran day and night until the liquid and solid wastes were removed. Fans pushed the funky air out and carpet blowers helped dry out the soggy mess over the next week. Then a chemical absorbent soaked up the residue and after a couple of weeks the crawl space was almost squeaky clean.

Evidently the extra fill used to create the crawl space had not been tamped properly and over time the soil began to settle like a box of corn flakes. The settling soil pulled the pipe inexorably downward, eventually separating the main drainpipe at the joint just below the framed floor. Curiously, the tension of the shifting soils threw the main stack out of plumb just enough so that what was discharged from above missed the pipe below. Fortunately, black vinyl had been laid down during construction, making the final cleanup a bit easier.

Wally S___ remembered that some kind of settlement was eventually reached – but between the builder and the owners, not the soil and the pipe.

Psychotic Remodeling

7
THE SCHEDULE

There should never be any confusion between the homeowner and the contractor regarding the schedule as long as one hard and fast rule is understood: *The project always takes longer.*

There are a few ways to avoid this:

1. Decrease the size of the project by at least 33% long after you've begun. Before paint, cabinets, and fixtures are installed, have the contractor write up change orders canceling the back end of the job. Quality may suffer, but it is the most sure-fire way to remain on schedule.

2. Reverse the rotation of the Earth for several days. This solution is not advisable if you live near the coast or if your home is built on stilts, as many scientists speculate that reversing the rotation will create giant tsunamis and hurricane-like winds across the planet. Unfortunately, it is difficult to find a contractor capable of doing this in a timely manner. Check with God for references.

3. Travel around the world continuously, heading east, for several days while your kitchen is replaced or bathroom is re-tiled. While this will not actually speed up the project, you will lose a few calender days of your life, which is preferable to staying home to fret.

4. Ask your doctor to prescribe a medication that will place you in a comatose state for the final few weeks of the job. Give a relative power of attorney. Remain heavily sedated until the punch list is done.

The following is a sample schedule for an imaginary project, a three-sided 400 square foot addition intended as a family room. The home is a simple 1950's two-story. The addition will have some built-ins, upgraded lighting, sliding doors onto the patio, and one wall of windows. Nice, but nothing fancy.

The construction details are fairly straightforward. Spread footings, conventional framing, scissor trusses and a gable end make up this simple box. One wall section of the back of the house will be "blown out" to access the addition. Very little work is planned in the existing house - only creating a sheet rocked entry to the addition. This imaginary addition is being built in a Mid-Atlantic state, so cold and frost is not a problem.

Before the project begins, the client should receive a chronological listing of the construction steps required to complete the project. Sometimes the schedule is filled in over blank calender pages. No matter what the format is, the schedule should be obvious.

The contractor or project manager or job superintendent will create this fictional time line, which is an imaginary sequence of real events arranged in chronological order. The schedule facilitates co-ordination among subs and suppliers, and gives the homeowner some construction guideposts as the project progresses. The homeowner needs this information to arrange for: 1) Payments to the contractor. 2) Stereo and furniture deliveries the day after completion. 3) Extended stays by out-of-town relatives in their newly enlarged home.

The schedule may read as follows:

10-6 Utilities staked.
10-7 Permit, site work.
10-8 Excavate. Open hole inspection.
10-11 Excavation complete.
10-12 Form footings.
10-13 Inspection.
10-14 Pour footings.
10-15 Form foundation.
10-18 Inspection.
10-19 Pour foundation.
10-20 Strip forms.
10-21 Waterproofing, perimeter drains.
10-22 Inspection.
10-25 Backfill.
10-26 Lumber pack delivery.
10-27 Framing. Demo siding as required.
10-28 Framing.

10-29 Framing (set doors, windows, exterior trim.)
11-1 Framing and exterior trim.
11-2 Framing and siding.
11-3 Electrical walk-thru, roofing dry-in.
11-4 Electrical rough-in.
11-5 Electrical rough-in, HVAC.
11-8 Inspections, roofing.
11-9 Roofing.
11-10 Insulation, gutters.
11-11 Inspections.
11-12 Stock drywall.
11-15 Hang rock.
11-16 Hang rock.
11-17 Inspection.
11-18 Fill and tape. Begin entry between old and new.
11-22 Tape. Finish entry between old and new.
11-23 Texture.
11-24 Scrap drywall. Deliver interior trim.
11-25 Thanksgiving.
11-26 Interior trim begins.
11-29 Interior trim ends.
11-30 Painters.
12-1 Painters.
12-2 Painters.
12-3 Painters.
12-6 Painters finish outside. Electrical finish. HVAC finish. Hardware.
12-7 Inspections. Drywall touch-up.
12-8 Carpet.
12-9 Punch list, drywall touch-up.
12-10 Final inspection, paint-touch-up.

From the schedule, it's obvious this project will be done well before Christmas. There are even a couple weeks for delays built in. No weekends are figured, and someone suggests that the schedule can be "tightened up" on inspection days, i.e. work proceeds around inspections.

Even though all of the subs on this project are experienced, capable, and fairly dependable, no contractor in their right mind would care to predict what really happens, especially before they've even begun.

WHAT REALLY HAPPENS

10-6 Utilities staked.

10-7 Permit, site work. Dumpster and san-o-let arrive.

10-8 Excavate. Excavators had problems on last dig. Don't show. Are running one day late.

Weekend.

10-11 Excavators promise to arrive today. They keep their word, but arrive ten minutes before sundown and park their equipment.

10-12 Excavators begin digging. Find apparent human bones and ashes in hole. Excavation halted. Reschedule concrete truck.

10-13 Archaeologist from local university and police arrive the next day. Further digging with a two inch trowel reveals 50 year old whiskey and liniment bottles, and evidence of a fire pit for melting lead and roasting meat. Turns out the plumbers who built the house were heavy eaters and hearty partiers. Digging resumes late PM.

10-14 Excavators dig to required depth. Engineers say soil is too sandy, and not acceptable for an addition. They won't be held liable should the new addition sink into the ground. Engineers recommend over-excavating another three feet and filling the hole with compactable soil. (The 50 year old home that has never moved mutely looks out over the dig.) Write up change orders.

10-15 Dig down three more feet. Find an abandoned septic system. Spend rest of day figuring out what to do. Write up more change orders. Reschedule concrete truck.

Weekend.

10-18 Yank out old tank, haul off. Order more fill. Excavators level fill and compact as required.

10-19 Open hole inspection approved! Five days behind schedule in the first week.

10-20 Form footings. Schedule concrete truck.

10-21 Footing inspection passes.

10-22 Pour footings.

Weekend. Hurricane Billy Bob dumps heavy rains into the hole all weekend. Hole fills with water.

10-25 Rain stops. Contractor spends all day pumping water from hole.

10-26 Hole dries enough to resume work next day.

10-27 Foundation crew sets forms and steel. Works in the mud, until dark, to get forms ready for inspection.

10-28 Training Day at the building department. All inspectors are in seminars. No inspectors available until tomorrow.

10-29 Inspector peers into now dry hole. Inspection approved. Reschedule concrete truck.

10-30 Pour foundation on a Saturday. (Concrete costs more on weekends.)

11-1 Strip forms.

11-2 Waterproofing, perimeter drains.

11-3 Waterproofing and drain inspection passes.

11-4 Backfill. Job is now two weeks behind schedule after one month.

11-5 Lumber pack delivered. Because of scheduling delays, the carpenters have started another job. Although it was a small job to begin with, there were numerous extras. Contractor demos siding, cuts rafter tails on exterior wall.

Weekend.

11-8 Job sits.

11-9 Carpenters begin. Install sub-floor and walls in same day. Begin roof.

11-10 Carpenters set trusses, sheathe roof, and begin fascia and soffit.

11-11 Carpenters do a great job – finish two days early.

11-12 Roofer arrives, "dries in" house so electricians and HVAC crews can begin.

11- 13 Contractor and owner complete electrical walk-thru with electrician. At the end of the walk-thru, all of the lighting has changed from the plans. Plus, owner requests electrician do additional work in existing house. Electrician points out that electrical inspector will require new service change. Write up more change orders.

11-15 Demo crew knocks holes in existing foundation to provide access for heating runs.

11-16 HVAC crew adds heat plenum and cold air return in one day. Newer furnace installed by previous owner simplifies installation of additional heat runs.

11-17 Change orders signed, electrician begins rough-in, service change, and additional work in existing home.

11-18 Electrical rough-in. HVAC inspection passes.

11-19 Electrical rough-in, service change.

11-22 Electrical rough-in completed.

11-23 Electrical inspection approved. Framing inspection flunks. Turns out the lumber company that supplied the trusses didn't include a "truss schedule" with a "wet stamp."

11-24 Spend all day getting a "truss schedule" with a "wet stamp."

11-25 Thanksgiving. No inspections.

11-26 Day after Thanksgiving. Second day of four day weekend. Building department closed for holiday.

Weekend.

11-29 Framing inspection passes. Job now four weeks behind schedule. Contractor insists this is normal. Insulation truck drops off insulation but no workers. Roofing crew arrives, hangs gutter. Roof is stocked with shingles.

11-30 Insulation crew arrives at 6:30 AM, finishes job in 1 hr., 40 min. Roofers begin shingling.

12-1 Insulation inspection passes. Terrible rains keep roofers home. No drywall delivery today.

12-2 Skies clear, drywall is stocked. No roofers. (First day of hunting season.)

12-3 Drywallers begin hanging rock.

Weekend.

12-6 Drywallers don't show. Something about problems with the Immigration and Naturalization Service (INS).

12-7 New pair of drywallers arrive, finish job.

12-8 Drywall screw inspection passes.

12-9 Drywall fill and tape. Contractor builds a dust wall inside existing home prior to "blowing out" wall to addition.

12-10 Drywall. Second coat of mud completed. Contractor begins demo. Inside the wall to be removed, contractor finds one abandoned asbestos covered heat run. Entry to addition cannot be relocated.

12-11 Contractor calls every asbestos abatement contractor in the area. Eventually, he finds one who can look at the job in a couple of days.

12-13 Hunting season over, roofers return, finish roof. Drywallers finish taping.

12-14 Drywall finishers spray texture in addition. Asbestos abatement specialists due in a couple of days. Roofing inspection passes.

12-15 Drywall scrapped out. Asbestos guys due any day now.

12-16 Job sits.

12-17 Interior trim delivered. Asbestos guy shows up to provide estimate, which equals the balance of the contingency fund, already depleted by over-digging the excavation and the electrical service change. The good news, he says, is he can begin in a week.

Weekend. Write up change order.

12-20 Trim carpenters tied up on another job, rumored to be a large custom. Will arrive any day now.

12-21 Job sits. Trim carpenters remind everyone they were scheduled to work at the end of November, not December.

12-22 Job sits. No trim carpenters.

12-23 Contractor pours patio. No trim carpenters.

12-24 Asbestos Abatement Company arrives. A team of workers dressed in Tyvek jumpsuits and booties hang plastic in the kitchen, induce negative pressure in the working areas, seal off the rest of the house, keep the asbestos wet, put everything in plastic bags marked "**HAZARDOUS MATERIAL**" and finish in time for homeowner to begin Christmas dinner.

12-25 Merry Christmas.

12-27 Contractor completes demo and frames the opening between existing home and addition. No trim carpenters.

12-28 Contractor drywalls the opening. No trim carpenters.

12-30 Drywall finishers begin to fill and tape new opening. Trim carpenters arrive, set up tools.

12-31 Drywall finishers apply second coat to opening. Trim carpenters work AM only, then leave to get an early start on New Year's party.

1-1 Happy New Year.

1-3 Trim carpenters finish.

1-4 Drywall finishers apply third and final coat on the opening between new and existing.

1-5 Texture crew arrives and sprays opening.

1-6 Paint is delivered, painters arrive.

1-7 Painters stain woodwork.

Weekend.

1-10 Painters seal woodwork.

1-11 Painters lacquer woodwork.

1-12 Painters mask woodwork, prime walls.

1-13 Painters spray walls and ceiling with selected color, "Terrazzo Mist."

1-14 "Terrazzo Mist" looks too dark to homeowners. Bad weather keeps painters inside. Painters cut "Terrazzo Mist" by 50%, contractor writes up change order.

Weekend.

1-17 Painters repaint walls.

1-18 HVAC crew installs heat registers, thermostat. Bad rains keep painters from working outside.

1-19 Painters begin outside. Electricians begin installing outlets and switches. HVAC final inspection passes.

1-20 Painters finish outside. Electricians hang fixtures. One fixture is on "backorder." Hardware arrives.

1-21 Carpenter installs hardware, adjusts cabinets, sets shelving. Electrical inspection passes.

1-24 Addition is swept and cleaned. Carpet has not yet arrived from mill in Georgia.

1-25 Drywall touch-up. Carpet is delivered. Had the addition been on schedule, the carpet would have been six weeks late.

1-26 Carpet layers install carpet.

1-27 Paint touch-up, final inspection approved. Job substantially complete.

2-28 Backordered fixture arrives.

3-3 Electrician installs backordered fixture.

3-22 Landscape crew repairs sprinkler system, regrades back lawn.

3-23 Landscape crew lays sod. HVAC crew charges up air conditioner.

3-24 Landscapers plant bushes.

3-25 Job complete.

Scheduling delays are inevitable, but there are ways to keep them to a minimum.

Know exactly what goes into a job before it begins. Windows, fixtures, and cabinets need to be ordered well ahead of time. Check with subs and suppliers for lead times. Work up a secondary schedule that indicates *what* needs to be ordered and *when* it needs to be ordered to keep the job rolling. A major remodel is like a freight train. It takes a while to build up some steam, but when it does get going the last thing anyone wants to do is make it grind to a halt waiting for materials to arrive.

Good subcontractors are also busy subcontractors. If they can't work because parts aren't in, you may lose your work window. This, of course, has a snow-balling effect on other subs and is the precursor to scheduling nightmares.

Although hardware is one of the last items to go into a project, it can't be ordered too early. Granted, it is difficult to stare into an excavation full of water and have to think about that "perfect knob." But it must be done.

Many homeowners wisely select hardware and fixtures with a classic, or timeless, appeal. Otherwise, the order may be hopelessly out-of-date by the time it arrives. Some hardware orders automatically filter through a nebulous network of warehouses. This Never-Never Land is also known as "Backorder." Once an order reaches here, the job is in trouble. In the old days, this meant a client or contractor would wait 6-10 weeks for a shipment to arrive. After 10 weeks, the customer was informed the order would ship in three weeks. Five weeks later, half the order would arrive. By the time the balance of the order came in, the homeowner had already filed for divorce or died from the stress of remodeling. Then the homeowner or survivors would only gain some perverse measure of satisfaction when the problem was transferred to probate court, which couldn't settle the estate because the invoice for the "perfect knob" wasn't in just yet.

Computers have changed all that. Within a few days, the contractor knows the product a) is ready to ship in a week b) is not available. If the answer is "b," this means there is no supply of the faucet or knob heavily advertised in showrooms, big box stores, and trade journals by national companies. The "order" goes to the factory. The "factory" manufactures "orders" when they accumulate. It's like going to the Village Inn and ordering bacon and eggs, and then have to wait for more orders to pile in because the chef can only make 50 orders at once. Order ahead of time or make a substitution.

Actually, the heart of the matter lies with inventory taxes, which prohibit manufacturers from keeping large stocks of items on hand. And the cost of warehousing large items is prohibitive. Some firms have a short (2-3 week) "lead time," i.e. the number of days between when an order is placed and finally delivered. Window manufacturers, for example, stock parts and assemble the finished product as orders arrive. The delivery dates of these mass-produced items are fairly predictable. But custom and designer house parts that are in sporadic demand arrive – sporadically.

Contractors want homeowners to think of them as the guy in the white hat who can fix anything and do it on time. Homeowners want to hear this at the start of the job, and enable the contractor to spout off random completion dates.

Many contractors and their subs, through years of customer relations, are adept at telling the client what they want to hear. In many instances, this is distinct from the truth. They say they will begin your project tomorrow morning, "no problem." What they aren't saying, is that in order for such an unlikely event to happen, they have to finish that day's work at a superhuman pace and blow off the big client who just called because of a one disaster or another on a different project. A follow-up call at 7:00 AM the day of their "arrival" confirms they won't arrive first thing in the morning, as you naively imagined, but later in the "morning." (They make a point of using the word "morning" in their excuse to give the appearance that they are still on schedule.) At the risk of belaboring the obvious, morning always turns into afternoon – and still no workers. This prompts the inevitable response, "after lunch." A couple of hours after lunch, you learn the guys had to "pick something up." The next excuse, of course, is, "We want to get started on it first thing in the morning, not at the end of the day."

Half of what you hear would be considered bald-faced lies by some people. Tradesmen, however, consider their responses to be part of a juggling act, and they are trying to serve the needs of their clients as best they can. Experienced contractors have good coping skills. They are experienced at explaining away problems. Homeowners suspect, for example, that politicians lie on a constant basis, telling their constituents what they want to hear so they can keep their jobs. Most of us have gotten used to it. Well, tradesmen aren't much different. In many ways, it's an industry standard.

I've known schedulers who have privately admitted they've told expectant homeowners all day long that "so and so" was on his way out, when they knew for a fact that his arrival was an impossibility because he had three prior stops. "On his way out" could mean a lot of things – the worker is getting fired in the morning, going to Mexico for a week, or headed to Duffy's for a cold one.

Contractors who have longstanding relationships with subcontractors can usually get the straight poop on who's showing up when. Homeowners who believe what they are told should make a note to get their blood pressure checked regularly as they are constantly stood up by construction workers.

The second part of the truth: Showing up a day or two late is typical in the industry.

In my early years in the business, I always parroted what I was told. "The painters will be here tomorrow. They just told me so." Soon enough, I realized I sounded like an idiot because when the painters didn't arrive (surprise surprise) I caught the heat from the owner. "But you promised they would be here today!" Now, when I convey scheduled arrivals to homeowners, I always preface it with the disclaimer, "This is what I've been told..."

One remodel proceeded nicely until the end of the job, when the painters gummed it up. After four or five days of, "We'll be there tomorrow," they finally arrived and got started. I had used this particular individual and his helper on a few jobs and had no previous problems with his work or his scheduling. At the end of the first day on the job (about a week's worth of work was involved) they told me they were headed to Mexico the next day. While they were gone, I scrambled to find another painter to finish a very nice master bedroom I had created in a beautiful old mansion. The good painters were busy, and a bad paint job was worse than no paint job. The original guys finished the job when they got back, but the whole job went south after the painters got through.

I'm always amused by the sections in "how-to" books that instruct owners to be sure to establish a schedule and make the contractor stick to it. This is fine if you hire one person or company for a week or two. But as the number of workers and materials increases, the things that go awry increase exponentially. If a three month project is finished in four months, most everyone in the business will marvel at the speedy completion.

I'll be quite candid here. Everyone talks about the schedule. Unless there is a specified completion date in the contract, I don't really care when the job finishes. I care that people show up every day, work efficiently, and do the very best work they can. I care that the customer has a quality job that everyone can be proud of, and that they didn't go through too much brain damage during the construction. But a year after we've all left, they'll forget it took a little longer if the quality is there.

To me, it doesn't make any sense to rush through a job to meet a schedule, then come back constantly after the project is "completed" to attend to all the little details that should have been done in the first place. Yet this is what some builders do and some homeowners demand. Working around furnishings and families takes twice as long – this makes the job drag out even longer, and becomes a continual source of aggravation to the homeowner. I think everyone knows quality takes time. The workers in your home will be like everyone else – imperfect. Give them a chance to redo a wracked door or a bad drywall joint. Just because they may not have figured in the time to correct some mistakes doesn't mean that you shouldn't.

I once hooked a toilet up to the hot water line by mistake. Thinking back on it, there were a few advantages. The bowl would have stayed cleaner and the seat and bowl had a more ambient, even cozy, temperature. But I'm sure it would have been hard on the flushing mechanisms and the utilities bill.

Lisa J___'s sprinkler guy accidentally hooked the lawn sprinklers up to the hot water. He called her that night after a couple of beers too many, feeling bad about how the day went, and promised to fix it in the morning. "But this way," he said, "you can water all winter."

After all, if we told you what really happens, would you hire us?

Lao-Tzu tells us ruling a big country is like cooking a small fish. If he had been in the construction business, he might have substituted "building a small addition" for ruling that big country.

The tiniest addition I ever built measured 5'x7' – 35 square feet. We were adding a steam shower to a half-bath, and moving one interior wall one foot. The end result was beautiful, but I didn't anticipate the scheduling nightmares created by such a tiny space.

More than two workers at once in this three-quarter bath meant people were tripping over each other. This severely reduced the number of man-hours available during the work week, and contributed to the job dragging on for a few extra weeks. (See Chapter Four, definition **b**, "clusterfuck.")

The home was constructed of solid masonry, which is tough to work with and resistant to change. She was a squat gray ranch, Mid-Century construction, decorated with some trimmed juniper bushes along her front porch and crabapple trees around back. We worked there in the fall and mashed the little fruits into the fresh mud with our boot heels every day. The demo and tear out was messy and nasty.

The owner was a great sport about the project, but couldn't reconcile all the tradesmen's scheduling guesstimates. "I'll be there today or tomorrow, depending on if the parts for Elm Street come in, and if I don't finish Friday I won't be back 'till Tuesday," with his own professional background.

Lou P___'s work world was a galaxy removed from the haphazard timing that dominates the construction field – he directed basketball and hockey broadcasts. Lou worked in a world timed to the second. He could look at a calender and know that at 7:15 PM on a certain date in three month's time he would be in Boston cutting to a commercial break. I, on the other hand, was trying to complete a job that should take only 6 weeks in 10 weeks if I was lucky. Most of the fixtures were on backorder, and I knew we would have to reselect everything at the end of the job anyway.

When the job was clearly not going to meet the first schedule (the fictional one) Lou took great interest in the updated schedule I provided every few days, and became mildly upset when the schedule required constant revisions. I was up front with Lou about some of the problems (inspectors requiring additional work, unforeseen problems in a confined space) and he seemed to accept the situation, but I sometimes envied the precision and timeliness of his profession.

I know that other professionals shake their heads in disbelief at the random arrivals and departures of the tradesmen on their homes. (Of course, I doubt if many of them are required to bail their workers out of jail to keep the project on schedule.)

If there is a choice between quality and timeliness – and there usually is – I will choose quality every time.

Sometimes there is a feature on a local newscast where an army of workers gets together and somehow builds a little tract home in a day as a stunt for a local charity. (Habitat For Humanity is closing in on the three hour mark!) I can't imagine what the finished product looks like – it's probably no thing of beauty – and comparable to a basketball game between two lousy NBA teams on a Wednesday night in the middle of February.

Psychotic Remodeling

8
I HAVE A
RECURRING DREAM...

It's a large house at the end of a cul-de-sac space. The building sits too high on the lot, and is way back. The proportions are...dreamlike. The concrete sidewalk that leads to the front door is steep and is full of treacherous steps.

This home is only a couple of years old, and the parts have been on order since before the move-in. I have worked there for a couple of days, off and on, but can't remember where this house is. I can't remember anything about the owner, although a dark-haired woman comes to mind. There is no paperwork. Although I'm positive I've worked there, I haven't sent a bill or gotten a check. I can't finish anything, because the parts come in only once or twice a year.

In my dreams, I sometimes drive into a cul-de-sac, but can't read the house number – it's too far away.

I drive a blue Ford pick-up and my name is Rick, AKA "Mac." If you are reading this and believe it may be your house, please notify the publisher.

Psychotic Remodeling

9
LANAI LAMENT

Terry B___ didn't even have a face a mother could love, although Alfred Hitchcock or Stephen King might have appreciated it. I hated sharing the elevator with him and his police sketch composite expression.

"Terry" was more than just a name. He was really a number – 806. I spent almost two years working in a 10 story, 80 unit condominium building. This structure was a lego-style collection of pre-stressed concrete and glass and metal panels, in the style of early Mies van der Rohe meets an Eastern European housing project.

The twenty-five year old galvanized water pipes had begun to corrode and the fellow I worked for was replacing the galvanized pipes with copper pipes. Each unit had two "risers," large pipes that fed the bathrooms and kitchens. The plan was to replace each riser and its branch lines one story at a time. Consequently, we spent over a year methodically working in everyone's "unit." Because the floor plan of each story was identical, we would tackle 203, 303, 403, etc. in sequence to complete each riser. My job in this methodical assault on a couple of hundred residents was to open up six one foot square holes in each unit so the plumbers would have access to the pipes, and then patch them up when the plumbers were finished. At our daily meetings we talked about every unit on that day's agenda. And though we came to know most of the residents by name, at first we only referred to them by their numbers. For some residents, that nomenclature just seemed appropriate.

But this was also for the sake of convenience. Not all of the residents became personal acquaintances. Still, it's impossible to work with people

53

for almost two years without forming attachments, especially when you spend all day with your head under their kitchen sink or behind their toilet. 806 was an imposing figure – at six feet three inches, he seemed to tower over me in the small elevator. His thinning brown hair was slicked back across his shiny scalp. His skin was perpetually glossy with an iridescent sheen. Like a portrait with lifeless eyes that follow someone around a room, I remember his bulging eyes always seemed to focus on me a couple of instants too long every time I stepped into the elevator. A wan smile or a direct "How are you doing today?" never evoked a verbal response – just a longer stare and a frown. In two years I only heard him speak once – to complain to the management in a thin, reedy, and belligerent voice. 806 only ventured out early in the afternoon to shop, usually at the corner liquor store. He always wore a black raincoat, a cheap one, sometimes over his pajamas. In the amplified silence of a claustrophobic elevator, his wheezing and coughing echoed like dirt clods on a coffin.

He was not well.

806 didn't live alone. "Mae" was his cousin, (or aunt) it was rumored. She was at least ten years older than Terry, around sixty, and certainly more sociable. Every now and then she came into the room the crew met in off the lobby and joked with us for a few minutes in her raspy smoker's voice. She had the air of a woman who was once cultured and educated, but those days were far removed from the Mae we came to know. When she was straight she was a joy – but when she was drinking she turned cold, and was known to parade around in the lobby with her shiny gold shoes on the wrong feet. She was slightly pigeon-toed, so when her shoes were on the wrong feet it produced the comical effect of her toes pointing in opposite directions beneath her undignified stupor.

Mae's hair color, like her personality, came right out of a bottle. It was bright red, and her makeup looked as though it was drawn on with markers every day.

My boss, "Frank," found her crawling through the hall late one day, drunk and bloodied, half naked, crying...

When we weren't punching holes in walls and changing pipes we were enclosing the balconies, called "Lanais," to create more year-round space for the condo owners. Lanai is a Hawaiian term for balcony. This was one of the few condos in the city that had a balcony off each unit – thus the entire building was aptly named "The Lanai," but we were hardly in Paradise.

We enclosed 602's balcony during our spare time, and it needed one final touch – a coat of acoustic spray on the ceiling. This was a cheap, mid-seventies way of covering the bare, painted, concrete ceiling. One afternoon, when his wife was gone, he ushered us in and told us this was to be a surprise for her. He arranged with my boss, "Frank," for the work to be done when he and his wife were out of town. We would have a week and a half to complete the job. No problem.

We were gutting 301 at the time, and we didn't get around to the balcony until the day they were due home. In retrospect, that was our first mistake. But we had done dozens of those ceilings, and they took less than an hour to complete if the balcony was empty, maybe two hours if there was a lot of furniture to move.

That morning "Frank" rented a sprayer. I taped everything off and hung plastic sheets from the ceiling to protect the rest of the apartment. We moved all of the furniture with great care, especially the famous 18th century Japanese tea table that boasted about 600 coats of lacquer. The reason it was so famous was that a plumber had accidentally scratched it with a length of pipe a few months earlier when we changed the risers in 602's "stack." 602 launched into a tirade at the next meeting of the condo association and rightfully demanded that the plumbing outfit pay for the costly repair job. Thus the extra precautions that morning.

One of the rules of the condo association was that no work in the building could begin before 8:00 AM. It was 9:00 by the time we hauled our equipment up, moved the furniture, hung the plastic, mixed the acoustic to a uniform slush and hooked up the sprayer. Even at this early hour, the temperature in our cellophaned workspace was already approaching 100 degrees. We had to keep all the windows closed because the slightest breeze would cause the thin plastic sheets to flap wildly. There was plastic everywhere, and we felt like we were working in an oxygen tent with no oxygen. The texture machine stood at attention, ready for work. Time was of the essence, so we fired up the compressor.

Ear plugs should always be worn with compressors because the noise is usually deafening, especially in a confined area like the one we were trying to work in. We didn't have any, and the incessant rattle bounced off the concrete ceiling and through our over-heated and oxygen deprived brains.

We loaded the hopper up and "Frank" balanced it over his head; working with precision the way we had in the past. He sprayed and I cleared the air hoses and cords out of his way and kept the goo going. The outfit "Frank" normally rented the sprayer from was out of them that morning, so he rented one from a different place. That was the second mistake.

I don't know what was wrong with it; probably the piston was shot and it was dirty too, but one thing was certain: after about three minutes, halfway through the ceiling it began to have seizures. It would either stop spraying and gurgle like an empty can of shaving cream or spurt the mud in an erratic stream like an oversized, orgasmic water pistol. So much acoustic collected on the lightweight plastic from the unsuccessful passes that when the sprayer gave one final heave, the resulting spurt tore through the plastic barrier and splattered runny cottage-cheese goop across the full length of the apartment.

We shut everything off, wiped our feet, and stepped out to survey the damage. But "Frank" slipped on the ever-present plastic, landed alongside the mixing bucket of acoustic and knocked it over with his head. Two gallons of glop ran over the floor, and about a pint of it was packed into Frank's ear. He stormed into the bathroom, leaving me to deal with the escalating crisis on the balcony.

I bundled up the plastic, threw it out, and sucked up the remaining mud off the carpet with the shop vac. Curds were everywhere. I wiped the tea table off fast, brushed the little white dots off the magazines, put the blemished ones on the bottom of the stack, and vacuumed and wiped some more until the place looked respectable.

One problem remained – a small charcoal sketch of a hand holding an apple that had borne the brunt of our assault. I didn't know the artist, but I doubt that he intended for his subject to hold a diseased fruit. Half-inch long blobs landed right on the apple. The hand was freckled with dots as well. I flicked the largest curd off, only to find we'd left it on the sketch long enough for the wet texture to absorb most of the charcoal beneath it.

We would hear about this.

There was only one thing to do. We found a soft lead pencil and carefully filled in the dots. It wasn't perfect, but it would have to do.

We broke for lunch, found a sprayer that worked, and went through the whole process again that afternoon: the plastic, the mixing, the spraying, and the cleaning. This time the job proceeded without a hitch and we were out of there in 45 minutes, working like demons and consumed by the fear that 602 and his wife might return at any moment.

I saw 602 in the elevator the next day, and he complimented me on the way his ceiling turned out, but, as was his nature, chided us about our cleanup job. He'd found, by his own count, four chunks of acoustic behind a cabinet. I apologized for the oversight and casually asked if he'd seen "Frank" yet. He said he had, but that "Frank" acted as if he hadn't heard a word he'd said.

Apparently 602 didn't know that "Frank" had already gotten an earful.

We also re-tiled bathrooms in the building at heavily discounted rates, but only to collect salvaged tile to patch the other bathrooms back together. Some of these tenants volunteered their used walls out of a sense of community spirit; on the other hand, the building was constructed with 80 units of 4x4 tile the color of milk chocolate pudding (master bathroom) or lemon meringue pie (powder room). So it's no wonder they would trade in the ugly stuff for something more suited to their personal taste.

It's strange to work in other people's homes on a constant basis – to wind your way through their furnishings, follow their paths. To move belongings in and out of their cabinets, know what they eat and drink, what medication and drugs they're on. I'm surprised when there are no books in a home, while some people live in a stifling clutter of teetering stacks of newspapers and dusty romances from years past. I don't understand why so many people leave their televisions on all day – evidently to keep the walls company. Others blast the stereo while they're watching TV.

You can't help but notice the old photos on the dressers and in the hallways, and piece together the family history of people you hardly know.

Answering machines sound off all day, making me privy to details I really don't want to hear. A critical parent chiding his 50 year old daughter, the bank leaving an urgent message, old friends sharing travel plans. The library saying, "the book is in."

The common floor plan of each unit only served to exaggerate individual taste and personal style. Behind the identical brown doors down identical brown halls on each floor were totally unique spaces as each owner created their world in their own vision. A corner apartment on one floor would be bright and airy, while the one below it might feel closed up and stuffy. If the surroundings we create are a reflection of the soul, I couldn't help but wonder about the lives of many of the tenants.

A few tenants had haystacks of magazines and newspapers everywhere. Their counters were cluttered with cheesy cups and containers they'd saved from fast-food outlets and convenience stores. Closets packed to overflowing forced them to stack more clothes on their floor and bed, leaving nowhere to sleep. These "hoarders," I later learned, were OCD's – victims of Obsessive Compulsive Disorders. But in the elevator and lobby they seemed like well-balanced people living typical lives.

The couple in 904 had an elegantly furnished apartment. Plush carpeting, mirrors, lots of glass shelving and chandeliers full of tinkly glass. They had a brand new bathroom of marble tile, courtesy of one of "Frank's" special deals. Lighted artwork graced the walls, every nook had a statue of a naked cherub, and there was a candelabra on the Baby Grand. The high powered telescope near the balcony wasn't for star-gazing. The snapshots of nude men we saw scattered around the place always generated quite a bit of discussion in the lunchroom.

The heterosexual male in 804, which was directly below, was at the opposite end of the decorating spectrum. 804 was handsome and dark-haired, always impeccably dressed in a suit and tie. He tooled around the city in a silver Jaguar convertible. Yet behind his brown door the apartment was stripped bare to the drywall. No carpet. Definitely nothing on the walls. There was one small formica table with wrought iron legs in the eating nook and a pair of matching chairs. The bedroom dresser vomited clothes and was piled to overflowing with loose change. The double bed was perpetually unmade. There were also a couple of plants – a rhododendron and a fern – that sprawled all over the cold gray floor, some of the leaves dried up and browned like old jerky. They looked like plants someone might have been dragging around since college. 806 was a private person, but our best guess was that he was a recently divorced attorney.

Successful professionals don't take time to make their beds, do their dishes, or dust their homes. In the morning, they are preoccupied with work. Their daily focus does not extend to housework, regardless of their sex. If there is no spouse or maid to unclutter their existence, it doesn't get done. The sharp image they project in their business world is often at odds with their housekeeping habits. Tidy professionals are the exceptions, and are usually at the top of the food chain – they don't have a 7:00 AM and 7:00 PM meeting in the same day.

730 had taken an early retirement because of his nerves. His apartment was brown and dark, the shades always drawn. Jim C___ used a very expensive stereo system to pipe elevator muzak into every room. The problem was, it was so mellow and dark in there that every worker who spent time in Jim's place was ready for a nap by the end of the day.

Progress was steady but slow.

Although we had more work than we could handle, 204 called late one night with a tiny side job. Bud ___ was a burly retired man with a little Yorkie who was the center of Bud's life. He sobbed that Charley was dead and wondered if we could make a pine box with a screw-on lid measuring exactly 16" by 10" by 8" high and bring it in that morning. It was not a problem.

Two young men lived in 504. Plywood wainscoting covered their walls, the carpet was long gone, and it wasn't a decorating statement. The only food in the house was usually scattered around the counters, the place smelled bad, and the refrigerator was usually empty except for white things: two or three jars of mayonnaise, milk, eggs. They were handicapped, wheel-chair bound, and making it on their own. Jerry, in fact, was one of the friendliest and most popular residents in the building. Jerry's father visited regularly and made a special point of taking us aside, passing out his card, and telling us to call him should anything come up. But Jerry's roommate moved out one day and then it was only a matter of time before Jerry left too.

304 was a used-car executive type, primarily known for shagging his girlfriend in the pool late nights.

The exhibitionistic young adults in 203 weren't about to let a crew of plumbers sidetrack their lovemaking. And what caused the panties of the fat lady in 603 to stick to the wall? And why did we have to see it? It was once the Topic of the Day.

Mrs. H___, a thin blonde with dark roots in 705, surely considered herself a "well-kept dame" for the last 30 or 40 years. Her friendliness level with all the workers always rose a few notches when her husband wasn't around. One day I startled her in her bedroom as I was finishing up that day's work in her bathroom. "There's a strange man in my bedroom," she squealed aloud to no one in particular. Aside from shards of tile and globs of mastic dotting my Levi's, I didn't think I was *that* strange.

George S___, 610, was a mild mannered Italian gentleman. A retired English teacher, he had slight stutter in his shuffle owing to some mysterious nerve disorder. His toy poodle's daily walks were good exercise for the both of them. On the days when 610's legs weren't up to the task, I remember him sitting in the lobby, wearing a cardigan and a pork-pie hat, stroking the little white dog on his lap. George was a delight to be around, always personable and well-informed about a wealth of subjects. We had

known him for several months before we found out this soft spoken, erudite gentleman was the black sheep of his family, which everyone knew as the city's most famous Mafia family.

There were a lot of guns in the building. Gun owners don't make any bones about letting workers know they have weapons and how they are prepared to blast away the next SOB that breaks into their home or hijacks their car. This can be a scary thought, especially for plumbers. Crime in that building was less than zero; it was in a stately old neighborhood (the Governor's Mansion was just down the street) but paranoia can fuel some powerful thoughts.

405 had a secret closet constructed especially for his gun collection. One wall was totally filled with built-ins. There was a wet bar in the center of the unit, and glass shelves above the sink for glasses and bottles. To the right was a stereo system and his vinyl collection, and on the left side was a bookcase. Behind the toe kick were casters. A three foot wide section of the bookcase was hinged, and opened out into the middle of the room. The books on the shelves were fake, purchased from thrift stores, cut at the spine, and glued together to give the illusion of greater depth. On the walls behind the fake shelves were 30-30's, AK-47's, shotguns and handguns. We built it, but we never said a word.

We knew where all the wonderful cooks lived, and who ate out of Hamburger Helper boxes. The musicians and the music lovers, workaholics and alcoholics, would pass each other not knowing how much they shared. We knew where the sickness was and where the skeletons were hidden. The building was a community, but of strangers under one roof.

The only apartment I refused to work in was 806, Terry and Mae's place. I made "Frank" work there. He said it wasn't too bad, sounding like the fellow who went over Niagara Falls in a barrel and lived to tell about it. My last recollection of Terry was the day I was heading down from the top floor. The elevator stopped on eight, the doors opened, and two paramedics wheeled and then tilted up a gurney into the small elevator car. I had never been that close to a body bag. It was another awkward instant with Terry, but at least we weren't alone.

Psychotic Remodeling

10

FORWARD TO:
THE TWILIGHT ZONE

Panoramic shot of new subdivision. **Long angle looking down.** The homes are one and two story, the streets wind in graceful curves. The only trees are newly planted and very small. Some lots are still empty and full of weeds. Small children play on the sidewalk. **Camera pans down** to a white service van with red lettering stopping in front of a single-story ranch home. **Medium shot.** A black-haired man in his late twenties wearing a blue service suit steps out of the van and walks to the front door.

NARRATOR

This is Mr. Phil H___, by all accounts a statistically typical American male. The first time owner of a brand new home, Mr. H___ is about to open a new chapter in the family saga. Mr. H___ doesn't know it, but this chapter will eventually surface in a place he could never imagine...

Unresolved issues sometimes swirl in eddies through the rooms and hallways of certain houses for no apparent reason. The oddest problems will cluster at one address while the home next door, built by the same crews and supplied by the same dealers, will be unaffected.

Possibly a majority of the work was scheduled on Fridays – or the owners are victims of a variety of unfortunate coincidences. Maybe the home was built on an Indian burial ground or in the middle of a cosmic vortex. I suspect some homeowners bring unseen and undefinable psychic baggage to their front door and, before they know it, live in a house that deviates from industry standards by a factor of THIRTEEN QUADRILLION.

Phil H___ and his family lived in such a place. Their development had undergone several ownership and name changes by the time I spent a year poking around their subdivision, embarking on my "New Home Repair" phase. The houses were drab and sad-faced, sitting around their cul-de-sacs in various stages of completion like wallflowers at a school dance, hoping someone might be interested in a walk-thru. It was the kind of sub-division Pete Seeger used to sing about.

Phil was in his late twenties, worked for a fire-sprinkler installation firm, and designed and installed commercial sprinkler systems. Consequently, he had some nuts and bolts experience assembling a structure. Phil was as puzzled as I was about the mysteries of his home.

Wall switches worked nothing. The wire running out of the switch box snaked through the attic, beneath the insulation, back down a wall cavity and into the basement, only to disappear through a cosmic anomaly called an "inter-dimensional bleed-through." I knew that as I flipped his switch half the day, someone in another time, another dimension, was probably complaining to some aggravated electrician that their ceiling light was going on and off for no apparent reason.

When Phil showered in the three-quarter bath water flowed unimpeded into his basement, splashing merrily onto the concrete at the rate of a gallon a minute, comparable to the flow of a hallway water fountain.

The unfinished basement's ceiling was wide open, allowing me a clear view of the pernicious water's pathways to puddles.

The drain was completely exposed – and clearly watertight with no leaks. To find the source, I worked from the bottom up. I filled the fiberglass shower pan with water from a bucket and everything stayed dry when I drained it.

Yet the floor joists were water stained, leading me to conclude the leak was higher up on the wall. But a thorough examination showed no obvious causes. The shower was less than six months old. The caulk joints at the base seemed ...OK, and there were no obvious holes in the grout.

Nevertheless, I cut out all the caulking with a razor knife, recaulked with a high grade of silicone caulk, and let it cure for a few days before retesting. (Note: A properly installed shower pan won't need caulking to keep it from leaking, but that's only in the real world.)

Retesting proved one thing; caulking was a waste of time. Water streamed out of the basement ceiling. The leak seemed to be worse.

I turned my attention to the valve. Common sense dictated that if the leak only happened when the water was running, it had to be at the valve or the pipe running up to the shower head. If the supply lines leaked, the water would run all the time. I opened up a hole in the drywall on the other side of the valve, in the wall common to the shower valve. Not a big hole, only large enough to satisfy my curiosity and watch water run out of the top of the shower valve when I turned it on.

No matter how much I flooded the basement, the valve and pipes were dry. In fact, they were *dusty*.

The source of the Nile was not as mysterious as this.

It was now becoming apparent that Phil H___ had the misfortune of purchasing a tract home inadvertently aligned according to some ancient previous life and, by some cosmic accident, I had to deal with his bad karma.

Homes can be exorcised for demons, just like humans. I was very close to consulting a "House Whisperer" when I finally discovered the source of the leak.

Tiny pin-sized holes in the one-eighth inch wide grout joints, visible only with a magnifying glass, provided openings for a network of rivulets that coursed between the back of the tile and the mastic it was embedded in. These tiny channels, the size of tear ducts, eventually coalesced into a raging torrent behind the tile at a point not too far above the shower base. I actually used a magnifying glass and a 300 watt bulb to find them, and then water-tested the innocuous holes with a garden hose to verify my conclusion. When I hosed them with a light pressure, the offending leak reappeared in the basement almost immediately. Scratching out the old grout and regrouting was a cheap fix compared to an exorcist.

One malaise this particular tract community suffered from was the Saggy Concrete Syndrome. The soil around many homes was never back-filled and tamped properly. Sidewalks, driveways, and front porches began to settle and crack during the first year. The front porch slabs always stayed attached to the houses, but the fronts of them dropped a few inches and the porch posts, still attached to the roof, flopped around at the bottom and swayed in the breeze.

It was a routine fix. I just called the mudjackers.

Mudjackers look like massive amphibious assault vehicles when they pull up to a house in a deafening hydraulic wheeze; a 10 ton truck with a 500 gallon tank of sand and cement mix, a water tank, air compressors, jackhammers, bags of cement, shovels, and enough feet of four inch rubber hose to circle the Empire State Building.

Mr. Mudjack will drill a four inch hole through the south-bound slab with a pneumatic hammer drill, push the hose down, and start pumping his grout mixture down the hole. Soon enough, the slab begins to lift up and the **CUL-DE-SAC ZONE** operator stops slab desired driveways, holes or more. lar develop- when the reaches the height. Big slabs, like may require half a dozen The porches in this particu- ment usually took two or three. An experienced operator can judge how many holes are needed and balances his lifts without cracking the existing slab. Mr. Mudjack then patches the holes with a special mix out of a five gallon bucket. He makes it look simple, but nothing at Phil's house was simple.

I knew this particular operator. We had worked on several identical porches previously, and Phil's house was just a replay of another day.

Wrong.

Mr. Mudjack had been pumping the first hole for about fifteen minutes before he looked at his watch with a puzzled expression. Once he started pumping, the noise level died down enough for us to talk about his next job, my next job, where the good fishing was, how the sports teams did that weekend, anything and everything. We lost track of time for a while, undoubtedly because of the disturbances caused in the time-space continuum.

He checked his gauges and said the pressure hadn't gone up. He shook his head when he said that must be a really big hole under there, because he's pumped five times the grout a typical porch requires. News like that always turns my eyebrows into a V and makes my chin jut, so we slowed it down a bit and started looking around the house, expecting to see grout oozing out the side of the slab or coming out from beneath it.

Nothing.

I knew Mr. Mudjack was ignorant of the bad "ju-ju" in Phil's house, so I motioned him to shut it off and we began to walk the now familiar path downstairs. Simultaneously Phil's wife, Theresa, ran screaming out of the basement. At the top of the stairs she managed to get out these words: "My foundation's caving in!"

That's always an attention-getter. We ran downstairs and saw all of the slurry we pumped had made its way into her basement. A massive pile oozed from the top of the outside wall and sprawled ten feet across the floor in all directions. There was no way this Blob could be integrated into any Feng Shui principles. It was swallowing all their positive Chi even as we gaped at it.

Though the basement was unfinished, her little kids played down there. A quick head count allayed our worst fears, but their colorful Play School benches, tables, crayons and toys poked out from beneath the gray "Blob." The framing lumber that circles the perimeter of a foundation, supports the outside walls, and holds the ends of the floor joists in place is called a "rim joist." Because Phil lived there, the rim joist mysteriously broke. The 2x10 couldn't stand the pressure and cracked along the grain between two joists. Then the sandy slime just kept on coming.

There were two good things about Phil's house. One, he had it upgraded to a walk-out basement with a sliding door during construction. I managed to get a crew out there almost immediately and wheel-barrow the mess outside to the empty lot next door before it set up. A front-end loader took care of the rest, and we were able to wash and mop and scrub and salvage almost all of the toys.

Number two, Phil never finished the basement. Garden hoses and shop-vacs restored the bare foundation walls to their original condition (cold bare concrete) with very little headache. Once the mud was cleaned off the walls, the foundation was fine. I double-blocked the mystery hole at the end of the next day, and we were able to pump up the offending slab a few days later with no problems.

I don't believe that porch has budged in the last twenty years, but I'm not going back to check.

11 CHANGE ORDERS

Throughout this text a couple of words keep resurfacing: Problems and change orders. Unfortunately, the two words are often wed, like ham and eggs. We will deal with problems later (sound familiar?) but for now let's get acquainted with change orders.

The setting is the living room of a newly remodeled home. The elegant lady of the house sits demurely on the flowered sofa as her harried husband paces back and forth. He is tall, dark-haired, and exceedingly well-groomed. The room was in shambles months earlier. Now it is brightly decorated and filled with sunlight. For many homeowners, this is the best day and the worst day. The house is finished. The bills are due.

The wife is Mrs. Blandings (Myrna Loy). Mr. Blandings is portrayed by Cary Grant, and the movie is *Mr. Blandings Builds His Dream House.* In the film, Jim Blandings leaves his New York apartment one day for a drive in the country and falls in love with a ramshackle home that was in its prime not long after the Revolutionary War. With eyes wide open and against all sound advice, he buys it and fixes it up. Mr. Retch is the general contractor on the project, and Henry Simms is the architect. In this scene, the tweedy architect leans on the fireplace, pipe in hand, and reconstructs the history of Mrs. Blandings' change order by a chronological listing of various bills.

Had the movie been filmed in color, Mrs. Blandings' face would be getting redder and redder as the bills pile up. Evidently Mrs. Blandings' innocent request has turned into a catastrophic change order:

ARCHITECT

$1247 – Changes in closet, Mrs. Blandings' little flower sink.

ARCHITECT, MR. BLANDINGS (IN UNISON)

You didn't authorize any changes, did you?

MR. BLANDINGS

What have you done?

MRS. BLANDINGS (DEFENSIVELY)

Well, all I did, was one day I saw four pieces of flagstone left over from the porch that were going to be thrown away because nobody wanted them, and asked Mr. Retch if he wouldn't just put them down on the floor in the flower room, and poke a little cement between the cracks and give me a nice stone floor where it might be wet with flowers and things. That's absolutely all I did!

MR. BLANDINGS

That's all you did!

MRS. BLANDINGS

Absolutely. Just four little pieces of flagstone.

ARCHITECT

Did you by any chance authorize a drain?

MRS. BLANDINGS

Of course I didn't. All I said was, "I wanted a nice, dry, stone floor" and Mr. Retch was as nice as could be, and said, "Well, you're the Doctor," and that was all anybody said about anything.

MR. BLANDINGS

Hmmmmm.....

ARCHITECT

Well, I think I can tell you what happened. First of all, the carpenters had to rip out the flooring that was already laid. These planks run under the entire width of the pantry. So, Retch had to knock out the bottom of the pantry wall to get at them. Then, he had to chop off the top of the joists to make room for a cradle. Ohhh...I guess he got some iron straps and fastened them to a large pan to give him something to hold the cement. And then, with that added load on the weakened joists, I'll bet he had to put a lally column down there for support, too!

MR. BLANDINGS

Hmph! I'll bet!

MRS. BLANDINGS

But it was just four little flagstones, and I –

MR. BLANDINGS

Quiet!

ARCHITECT

Retch had to get a plumber back and take out a section so that he could get the cradle set, and I'll bet he had to change the pitch of that soil pipe from one end of the house to the other! And of course there are hot and cold water pipes hooked to the joists right under that pantry. They run to the bathroom on the second floor. And reroute about sixty feet of armored cable between the main panel and the junction box by the oil burner, including the 220 volt cable that goes to the stove! Well, that's about the size of it, except that Retch had to repair the pantry wall, and that meant getting the plasterer back, and he couldn't have possibly broken through that wall without –

MR. BLANDINGS

All right Henry, all right, we'll take care of it!

ARCHITECT

I'll admit, it's a little steep, but I'll try to get Retch to knock $100 off the bill. If I can't get that, I'll certainly try for $75.

MR. BLANDINGS

Fine!

ARCHITECT

If he doesn't go for $75, I'll make stab at $50.

MR. BLANDINGS

You do that!

ARCHITECT (leaving room)

Anyhow, I'm almost sure we can get $25. Good day!

MR. BLANDINGS

Good day!

That $1,247 "change order" in today's dollars would be around $20,000.

Many owners wish they were like Cary Grant at one time or another, but no one in their right mind would want to be in Mr. Blandings' shoes. In the first place, his contract with Mr. Retch should have included the Prime Directive: *No changes shall be made unless they are authorized in writing with a signed change order.* Also, Blandings' architect should have driven up to the job at least once a month and noticed workmen changing the pitch of the main drain, tearing out walls, and adding structural columns!

Mr. Retch should have presented the Blandings with a nice clean piece of paper that said something like this:

Add floor sink in the flower room. Tear out floor as required, run new drain, and patch walls and floors as required. Notch floor joists to accommodate new cement pan and reinforce structure as required. Relocate utilities as required. Floor shall be constructed of four stones as specified by Mrs. Blandings.

This change requires 10 additional working days. All work to be billed as time and materials, plus profit and overhead. Estimated cost, $20,000.

The dollar amount on this change order is estimated. Because time is of the essence, it's sometimes difficult to get carpenters, electricians, plumbers, plasterers, masons and painters to come in and refigure costs with little or no notice. In this case, Mr. Retch gets as many costs as he can and estimates the rest. If Mr. Blandings refuses to sign off on estimated costs, then the job might shut down for a while as Retch tallies the cost down to the penny. In the absence of an accurate figure, Retch could supply a price range, say between $18,000 and $25,000.

Maybe then it wouldn't seem like four little old flagstones and the Blandings could have saved some serious money by placing them in the flower garden.

Of course, if this was the real world, Jim Blandings could have gotten out of paying anything because he never authorized it in writing.

Contractors are obligated to build to the plans and what is specified in the contract. While they may offer suggestions and point out practical matters if the plans are poor, they often reach a point where they don't feel they should be doing the architect's job. Incomplete and inadequate plans and specifications generate lots of change orders as the job progresses. Homeowners who skimp on money in the design process often lose those savings in change orders. Many homeowners mistakenly believe contractors like change orders to pop up on the job, and actually encourage change orders through surreptitious means. This is not entirely correct.

Change orders typically arise from a few different sources.

There is the Santa Clause. This is a surprise uncovered during construction that no one could have foreseen and is usually found behind walls and under the ground. Dry rot, abandoned plumbing, and wiring that has to be moved typically fall under the Santa Clause. For remodelers, it's a dollar and cents gift that has to be dealt with in a timely manner by the homeowner and contractor. Santa Clauses add time and dollars to the contract and are – innocent. They are no one's fault, they are a fact of life, and the reason contractors include contingency fees.

There is the "Might as Well" syndrome. Homeowners like the new windows in their addition so much, they want all of the windows in the house replaced. As long as the hardwood in the new kitchen is being finished, the rest of the house should be refinished. Since the electricians are running two new circuits to the basement, we might as well have them add outside lights and rewire the garage. "Might as Well" change orders are not critical to the performance of the contract and make the job run longer. Most homeowners don't seem to realize this until they refer to the schedule and realize electricians are still traipsing through their bedroom and sawing little holes in the walls when the job should be over. Many subcontractors who are scheduled out a month or two in advance are reluctant to go back for additional work. This creates scheduling conflicts that snowball or delay other jobs, so it's always best to plan extra work outside of the contract way ahead of time to avoid on the job hassles. Depending on the current state of the local building economy, many contractors don't pursue extras; in fact, many are just trying to get the job done in as speedy and professional a manner as possible so they can move on to the next project.

Homeowners who include the "Might as Well" phrase in conversations with their builder need to realize that many contractors have a congenital condition that doesn't allow them to refuse work. This condition causes them to nod their heads as though they had springs for necks anytime someone asks them if they can do this or that. If you are a homeowner, and suspect your contractor may have this condition, be sure to pin him down to a time frame and have a back-up plan should things not pan out. Most builders are eager to please and make extra cash, but many are stretched too thin, and they may not always be the best choice for the additional work.

The third set of circumstances that creates change orders rankles homeowners the most.

They are generated because the plans and specs are incomplete, inadequate, or unclear. The owner resents paying change order fees for work he felt should have been included in the original budget. If this is the case, the builder fairly or unfairly tries to deflect blame to the architect or whoever was responsible for the plans or any oversight. If there is a legitimate misunderstanding, and the additional work doesn't involve too much extra figuring, the contractor may reduce or waive the change order fee. When a circumstance like this arises, it is a good time to review the entire project for similar surprises.

A contractor may see "unfinished" areas on a set of plans and logically not bid any work. "Unfinished" may apply to a room, a closet, or an exposed foundation wall. Homeowners need to review their plans to ensure that "unfinished" doesn't mean, "I haven't made up my mind yet."

The painting bid for a client overly concerned about costs may be minimal on paper to keep the project within the budget (one paint, one color) and then inadequate (in the homeowner's) mind once it is on the walls. Painters will testify that the application of paint to the walls is only half their job. A great paint job, especially in an older house, demands lots of time-consuming prep work. Homeowners need to ask themselves how much time and money they want to invest in this particular line item.

In the pecking order of a job, painters don't get nearly the respect they deserve. Owners who seem to think they can get by with a cheap paint job are usually disappointed. (These are the same owners who want everything painted yellow, a color that experienced hands know takes twice as much paint to cover than any other color.)

In an addition, for example, landscaping is rarely figured into the budget. Only positive drainage. Landscaping is a separate (and sometimes expensive) category.

Extensive prep work may not show on the plans; prep work like tearing up an old floor to make two floor levels consistent. An architect may have mis-measured an existing window and not realized it will soon fall in the middle of a new wall. Architects usually include a disclaimer with their plans. The fine print says that all measurements are to be verified by the contractor. Depending on the scope and complexity of the project, this is often impossible, and dealing with changes from the original plan is a normal part of the remodel process.

(A fellow remodeler explained to me how he snagged a nice addition with one day of unusual preplanning. The whole point of the addition was to provide new space and enhance the view of the mountain range to the west. So the client spent one morning seated on a high stool at various locations in her back yard and the contractor's crew carried an empty frame around the lawn. This frame was the size of the window unit planned for the proposed addition. Once the homeowner visualized how everything would fall into place, the contractor got the job!)

Architects can be human, too, and make mistakes – often of omission. Their failing, however, is that they blame the contractor. "He should have picked that up," is a common phrase.

If conditions uncovered during construction require design changes or modifications, an architect or structural engineer may have to provide additional drawings for the builder or the building department. In this case, the owner typically pays for additional drawings. Where does this money come from? Contingency fees. Usually I make engineering a line item and plug in a realistic dollar amount in the allowance column.

Homeowners walk through their new home, show off the old trim, and try to hire someone to move one wall and patch the rest of the upstairs. Their plan might be to eventually wallpaper a new bedroom in an old house. They anticipate a small job. The owner sees "quaint and charming." The contractor sees disaster. First the old plaster begins falling off the old lathe in chunks the size of pizzas. The old trim – covered with lead paint. Behind the plaster – no insulation. In the walls, outdated and dangerous wiring. The framing is a carpenter's nightmare – undersized lumber spanning too great a distance. Before long, a simple wallpapering job can turn into a major undertaking without proper planning.

The owner of a picturesque beach cottage found this out the hard way. He wanted to make the place habitable year-round by adding heat. But after learning the walls and floors had to be torn up to retrofit the home, he decided to add a small addition. Then he learned he had to replace the existing foundation. Eventually, the size of the house doubled. At the top of his wish list – maintaining the original style and materials of the old structure that had withstood dozens of hurricanes and Nor'easters, but eventually succumbed to a legion of contractors and inspectors.

Code issues also generate change orders that upset homeowners. Once an inspector begins walking through an old house, he may require the owners to update or repair code violations in the existing home. It's impossible to outline all of them on a plan, and even predict what may be "grandfathered" in or not. Homeowners sometimes think the contractor knows about minor and major violations that need to be corrected and doesn't write them up until the job is underway in order to keep the original bid low. In fact, contractors wait until the inspector points them out, because what does and doesn't fly with the building department may be subjective and vary from inspector to inspector. If there is a real concern about a problem spot, like existing stairs, railings, or headroom, consult with the building department before the project is underway. Extensive remodels (50% or more of a residence) are inadvertently discouraged by local codes. Bringing an old structure up to code is the same as fitting the proverbial square peg into a round hole. The building department can force a homeowner to whittle away all of the original character and charm that made the house attractive in the first place. If the plan is currently under review they will usually provide feedback before it turns into a big issue down the road.

Unfortunately for remodelers, most local codes were developed with new housing in mind, not re-habbing and retrofitting 100 year old Queen Annes. Code uncertainties lead to cost uncertainties on major projects, scaring away investors and ultimately dooming old homes to a fate equal to death – a "scrape-off".

Construction codes, however, have been changing over just the last few years. Some municipalities have begun to loosen restrictions enough to encourage restoration, especially of historic structures.

There are a variety of reasons some homeowners don't pull permits on their jobs.

One, the work is minor and dealing with the building department over glorified repairs doesn't make sense to them. (Where I work, a permit is required to patch over 2 square feet of drywall. A permit is required to change a garbage disposal. To most homeowners and contractors, this doesn't make sense.)

Two, the contractor has warned them that once the building inspector begins to walk through this house there's no telling how much extra work he will require. Inspectors keep an eagle eye out for electrical code violations that can start fires. Unsuspecting homeowners who thought they were eliminating a closet can suddenly find themselves paying for a new electrical service! Homeowners should expect inspectors will review smoke and fire detection devices, and make sure that basements and attics that have been converted to living spaces have proper egress in case of fires. Homeowners spend more time consulting Martha Stewart than the Uniform Building Code when they are making their decorating decisions (and why not?) but once an inspector is on the property, his job is to enforce public safety, collect revenue for The Department, and inform the tax assessor of substantial property improvements.

Finished basements, especially in older homes, can look like firetraps to a building inspector. No windows in kids' bedrooms are common, and sometimes the ones that do have windows also have security bars.

(An old house with a small attic was a rental property for many years. When ownership changed, I spent some time patching and upgrading the property. The previous tenants kept their kids' bedrooms in the attic. It was a serviceable sleeping area for little kids, but the parents put a deadbolt on the door at the bottom of the stairs to keep them in at night. Bad idea. That was a tragedy waiting to happen.)

Common sense dictates two turn-of-the-century living spaces won't blend easily together – especially if they're from different centuries!

Mr. Retch has his own way of handling change orders. I have mine. In a perfect world, I'm happy to get one started early. There are usually one or two Santa Clauses at the beginning of a project and this is the optimal time to lube up the change order process. (Unfortunately, on additions they usually begin as soon as the hole is dug.) Most change orders have three copies. The original goes to the job file in the construction office, along with the signed contract. A second copy is for the homeowner's records, and the third stays on the job with the superintendent.

The change order should also specify how payment will be made. Many fall under the aegis of the regular payment schedule as outlined in the contract, but some may require a separate payment. The contract should clearly spell out change order costs and procedures. Owners may be be charged $25 to $100 per change order, plus time and materials, plus profit and overhead. A typical contract may say, "changes shall be made at cost plus 20% or cost plus $75.00, whichever is greater."

Contractors charge for change orders for a couple of reasons. In the first place, it takes time to estimate work. Sometimes the job needs to be stalled to implement a change order, which is costly to everyone. Also, a flat price or fee discourages homeowners from concocting senseless changes every night long after the job has begun. Without a fee for changes, some owners would request almost daily changes.

Change orders may also specify how much time is added to or deleted from the schedule, if a completion date is included in the contract. Upgrading carpets won't affect the completion date, but substituting cedar shingle siding for simple lap siding would obviously be more time consuming and add a certain number of days to the completion date.

I'm usually reluctant to write up "Might as Well" change orders in the early stages of a big project because all of the fixed costs may not be in. I think cost-conscious homeowners will wait until the inspector has seen everything before committing significant dollars to extra work.

It is common to have several change orders on a major remodeling project, with equal representation from all three categories. When the contractor has to figure extra costs, homeowners should realize they have given him an opportunity to make up for unforeseen expenses he has incurred in other phases of the project. The contractor may feel they are legitimate costs, but doesn't care to create ill will with his client by trying to recover dollars for what he should have picked up in the first place.

Less scrupulous contractors will know they have a homeowner between the proverbial rock and a hard place and try to take advantage of the situation with inflated costs.

And clients who hire a contractor to tear out and redo perfectly acceptable work because they have changed their mind(s) during the course of the job are simply wasting money.

Many undefined line items of the budget are considered "allowances" (See "Problems" Chapter). After these are selected, the owner will have a good sense of the final dollar amount, how much extra they can afford to spend, and how much longer they are willing to undergo the joy of remodeling.

Let's not forget one crucial point – change orders can also save money if the client wishes to eliminate or downgrade some work. If the owners want to do their own painting, for example, the dollar amount allotted for paint and labor is credited back against the balance owed on the final bill.

Note: These guidelines go out the window when the client's net worth exceeds that of a small third-world nation, which is sometimes the case. Owners with substantial resources know what they want and the contractor's job is to deliver it. But they too want to know, "how much?" and "how long?"

No matter the resources of a homeowner, any deviations from the original proposal must be dealt with promptly and properly. Leaving change orders to be signed off until the end of a job will almost certainly leave a bad taste in the client's mouth and reflect poorly on the contractor.

Psychotic Remodeling

12

MONTANA MIKE

Mike O'___, a tinner, used to live in a small cabin in the Montana woods with his first wife. By Mike's account, the cabin and his wife were both fixer-uppers. The house was trim and tidy, unlike his wife, who had been bugging him for years to finish the living room. Mike half-hearted-ly agreed with her, but the cost of rural living was that Mike had little free time on his hands. When he wasn't installing heating systems during the day he was stocking wood for the winter, mending fences, winterizing his house, or just plain tired from working his job 40 plus hours a week.

Eventually, Mike's life got settled and he ran across a good deal on some beautiful yet very green rough-sawn pine from the local lumber mill. He spent a couple of weekends that summer planking the walls, and was truly pleased with the final result. Although he conceded he was a better tinner than a carpenter, his wood-butchering skills and his home's rustic decor blended perfectly. The aroma from the green lumber was heavenly, flooding the entire house with the scent of fresh-hewn pine. When Mike and his wife hit the hay at night, they closed their eyes and imagined they were deep in the forest under a canopy of pine needles. Even his wife was pleased for a while and their wrangling died down some.

When the Montana winter began to set in, it was time to fire up the pot-bellied stove, fueled with the scrap of that summer's home-improve-ment project. An Arctic front dipped down the first week of October, sending temperatures into the single digits. Mike had spent a lot of time sealing up drafts, the ceilings were low, and the place heated up in no

81

time. Soon enough, the little cabin was downright toasty.

The home had a back-up oil-fired boiler; (Mike always thought it ironic that his place never had forced air) but they relied on wood heat most of the time because it was plentiful and cheap. Montana winters are brutal, and much of the year was spent preparing for them. One good thing, Mike and his wife could forget about the Concorde-sized mosquitoes, gnats, and beetles that plagued them all summer.

When his wife had the gumption to complain about bug-bites that week, he figured she was only giving him ammunition for divorce court ("Judge, she thinks mosquitoes bite her all winter!") and didn't pay much heed. When she showed him red welts all over her arms and legs, he reckoned she was psychosomatic. When bugs started dropping out of his beard and into his morning coffee, he ran to the mirror to check his hair. As soon as he turned the light on, a cloud of insects descended on the globe. To his horror, swarms of bugs and beetles were literally crawling out of the woodwork, on the counters, across the floor, and all over the lights.

Turns out the paneling was chock-full of dormant critters, eggs, and larvae of every species under an inch that calls a pine tree home. Cranking up the heat that last weekend only motivated a winter hatch *en masse.*

Mike set off a couple of bug bombs to take care of the insects, and hired a divorce lawyer to handle his wife's bugging.

13. PROBLEMS

It is never appropriate to shoot the plumber, although many home-owners and contractors have felt like Mississippi Man at some point.

All remodeling jobs have problems. Yours will, too! The process of remodeling is a process of problem solving.

Some of the variables are the size, duration, and cost of the problem. If your project is well-run, you may not be aware of most of the problems. The project superintendent's main task is problem solving as he schedules workers, inspections, and deliveries; mitigates cost overruns; works around the weather; and deals with challenges and secrets the home grudgingly reveals during the course of the project. (Rotted lumber, hidden water damage, out of level floors, etc.) It is often not in the best interests of the project if homeowners are informed of every little problem and hassle that crops up. There are just some things a homeowner doesn't need to know. Contractors and tradesmen are used to dealing with on-the-job hassles on a daily basis. Many homeowners, especially the ones that haven't read this book, have no perspective on the glitches that can make up a day on the job. Bad subs can torpedo good jobs by reciting a litany of complaints to a nervous homeowner. *Some subs just like to bitch and complain on the job.* This serves no purpose other than to soothe their own screwed-up egos. Homeowners who hear more than they need to can lose confidence in the builder and begin to obsess needlessly about routine problems.

During the interview process you don't need to ask the contractor's references if there were any problems. Instead, ask how problems were resolved. Were the solutions satisfactory to the homeowner and contractor? Did the client feel screwed? Were problems shunted aside to fester and grow? (Does the homeowner gloat about screwing the contractor?)

One of my tactics when a large project begins is to "red flag" certain areas I'm especially concerned about, whether they are underground drains, or site access, or potential material shortages and delays. I keep subs and homeowners (if necessary) apprised of my concerns and basically just try to stay on top of these items before they become an issue.

Typical recurring problem areas that homeowners need to to deal with: Design issues, costs, and level of workmanship. The "pop-top" won't fit in the "bulk-plane." The only place for the bedroom in the basement is in the northeast corner, and we can't provide egress from that area because there is a garage and front porch at the grade level. If we move the toilet a scant four inches to fit the new shower in, we'll wind up changing the drains in half the house!

Problems that stem from design issues also tend to have a negative impact on the budget. It is imperative for the homeowner, architect, and contractor to think the whole job through *before work begins.*

Homeowners who rely on architects to develop a set of plans for contractors to bid upon can expect to go through lots of paper. First, the architect and owner put their heads together to develop a set of preliminary drawings. These will indicate a basic floor plan, a site plan (how the addition, for example, relates to the rest of the property), and elevations, which show the completed project from different directions (north, south, etc.)

It's not unusual for homeowners to go through more than a couple of architects during this process. If the homeowner and architect haven't achieved a certain comfort level with each other during this design phase, it may be best to move on and have a new design team take up where the first one left off. *All parties need to be very clear about what level of drawings are provided during the preliminary phase and how much this work costs.*

Preliminary drawings will evoke only a "ballpark" response, at best, from contractors who are expected to price preliminary drawings. But after the preliminary design has been agreed on, the next step is a set of architectural drawings, "Builder's Plans," that clearly delineate the work at hand. In new construction, architects charge by the square foot. This square foot price will vary for remodel projects, depending on their complexity, so it's important to know what a complete set of plans will cost after the first meeting.

Owners who spend time and money at the front of the job on complete plans will realize savings at the end of the job.

Remember, "A doctor can bury his mistakes, but an architect can only advise his clients to plant vines." – Frank Lloyd Wright.

Homeowners considering a major remodel who feel good about their choice of contractor sometimes sign contracts – "Professional Services Agreements" – essentially hiring "their" contractor to pull together a design team comprised of architects, engineers, designers, and tradespeople to invest time and money into detailing a major project. This is always a worthwhile investment for owners who are serious about getting their project underway and willing to make an early financial commitment to getting the project started on the right track. Design/Build firms who can pull together a design team can anticipate big problems on big jobs.

Most clients have little practical experience reading blueprints. Many homeowners don't acknowledge their lack of expertise to the contractor because they fear they will be taken advantage of. If this is the case, wise homeowners will ask their architect to hold their hand as they walk them through their plans. Homeowners, remember this: The architect or designer is your advocate. You are paying them. There is usually a lot of money at stake here, and no question is stupid.

Contractors won't know Grandpa's portrait *has* to fit in *this* nook with *this* amount of clearance, or that wiring is required to light the portrait, *unless they are told*. They aren't privy to the size of your couch or the height of the side table that was supposed to fit under the window instead of in front of it.

Homeowners: Pay attention to those little squares that jut out from the wall. Pat C___ was a very bright and capable homeowner who didn't understand why an architect would design a wall in his new addition that would place a structural steel column inside the room instead of inside the wall. The end result was a 12" x 12" bump-out from the wall. It wasn't until the framing was complete that Pat noticed this "error" in the plans and insisted construction halt until it was corrected. This was not going to be an easy fix. The column supported a steel I-beam that was 18" high by 28' long, and spanned across the side of the new addition that was up against the original house. The offending "bump-out" was under that beam, where the new house met the old. I was the project superintendent, and assumed Pat knew what his addition was going to look like, as we built from the plans. Things were a little sticky because Pat C___ had some business dealings with my boss, the general contractor.

Here's what happened: We got a solution from the structural engineer and the job sat while a steel column narrow enough to fit into a 2"x 6" wall was delivered. The site was in the forest and it was impossible to get a boom truck in to drop off the new column, so we found a welder with a forklift to negotiate around all of the trees in the front yard. The hill in back was way too steep. We took a few feet of siding and sheathing off and opened up the outside wall. Then we jacked up the beam after the welder cut loose the original column. These columns weighed about 300 pounds. After it was freestanding, we wiggled column #1 out of the wall and pushed it outside. The ground shook when it hit. Then we walked column #2 into the opening from the inside of the house, set it in place on the foundation, bolted it tight, and lowered the horizontal beam back onto the column and welded them together. Had column #2 been a fraction of an inch wider, it would not have fit in the wall. But it did, and the wall and Pat's dander were eventually smoothed over.

Total charge to the client: Zero dollars

If Pat C___ didn't have a "special" relationship with the contractor, this fix would have generated a change order that ran into the thousands.

Pat's "problem" was less of a migraine than many others because the project was still in the framing stage. Fixing design misunderstandings after the client moves in takes twice the effort.

But small design issues can rankle a homeowner as easily as the big things. Homeowners who spend extra money and time on their projects, (i.e. "high-end") are usually unaware they've left the selection and location of basic home parts like air grilles and downspouts to tradespeople. Consequently, in the most democratic of gestures, suppliers and HVAC contractors furnish the same $10 grille to every home, should the room cost $10,000 or $100,000 to build. The problem is, that $10 cold-air return grille looks shabby when set in place next to $30,000 worth of built-ins. Upgrades and possible changes in the location of one or more grilles should be discussed before the project is in the framing stage. Custom grilles of wood and "special order" cast iron are available, but are not something that falls off the shelf in a timely manner.

Most owners assume gutters and downspouts should be engineered to collect rainwater and snowmelt from the roof and carry it away from the house. On a good day, this is what happens. But if the roof is complicated, with lots of hips and bays and bump-outs, the potential exists for the final result to resemble a Rube Goldberg creation, a complicated series of tiny gutters and extended runs of downspouts crisscrossing everywhere. These downspouts can snake around brick wainscoting, cover window trim, and fall in front of picture windows. They can even run across driveways and drain where they shouldn't. Remember, aesthetics are a minor concern to the installers. They are preoccupied with code requirements, making sure the gutters are properly pitched and don't leak, and moving on to the next job. The beautifully rendered architectural creation the owner sees before construction begins has no indications of gutters and downspouts. (Most architects don't do gutters.) Check with the contractor before the plans are finalized, and ask where the downspouts might fall. When making this assessment, also consider site orientation. Are there too many downspouts planned on the north side? Will these create ice problems every winter? Do these drain over sidewalks, creating hazards? It's important for the homeowner to address these issues, because they are rarely more than a blip on anyone else's radar screen.

Imagine standing in a beautiful new $50,000 kitchen. The cabinets are semi-custom and the countertops are granite. A casual observer might assume a lot of thought went into this project, and that observer would be 1000% correct. It reflects the best efforts of the architect, designer, builder, and craftsmen that built the entire house. This home has been honored with national design awards.

Then, why is it the day before Thanksgiving and the kitchen island and surrounding floor are littered with the tools of my trade? Drills, toolboxes, extension cords, granite saws with diamond blades, buckets of water, black pipe and gas fittings, electrical supplies and bx cable, a demo saw and a jigsaw, a shop vac and tarps, cover everything. All of the pots and pans stored in the island are piled on the kitchen table and large custom drawers are stacked at the end of the island.

Guess what. The cook top is too small to accommodate those large pots and pans. The owners didn't think through what they really needed when they selected appliances. The burners are too small to generate sufficient heat for the wok and too close together to center the large pots on the burners. Not only is the cook top being replaced, but the space age hood that rises out of the counter top has to be changed too, to fit the new and bigger cook top. The paneling on the back of the island has been removed to install the new duct work. Gas lines and vents need to be rerouted. Experienced as the design team was, no one thought to question and scrutinize the homeowner's selections. The drawers were mammoth, carefully sized and constructed by a meticulous cabinet-maker. The cook top? The owner selected it out of a catalog. Appliances usually go in at the end of the job, a few days before the owner takes possession. This owner moved in the weekend before Thanksgiving and panicked as she put her kitchen in place. Removing and replacing the cook top turned into a two day project and cost an extra two thousand dollars. The original installation took about two hours. We'll save the shallow sink for another day...

Losing track of "allowance" items is a common problem that affects the budget. An allowance is a dollar figure plugged into the contract for the purchase of unspecified items. In the contract, it might read something like this: *An allowance shall be an estimate only and the owner shall be responsible for any increase or receive a credit for a decrease in its cost.*

Most contractors routinely leave an allowance number for lighting fixtures, for example. In the old days, a single ceiling fixture with two 60 watt bulbs was considered adequate lighting for a room. That's all changed. Now, lighting is on tracks, recessed, and under-cabinet. There is up-lighting and down-lighting, task lighting, step-lighting, rope-lighting, mood lighting and puck-lighting. Bulbs are fluorescent and incandescent, flood and halogen and low-voltage. On every other job, we need to find a special home for the black, bulky, heat generating low-voltage transformer that has become an essential component of today's modern lighting requirements. Switches and dimmers have built-in microprocessors and are touch-controlled. Ceiling fans and lights can have remote controls.

If your project calls for twelve recessed cans and four wall sconces, suppose the line item indicates an $800 allowance – $50 per item. This might seem adequate at first. It looks good on paper, and may play its part keeping the bottom line on the contract manageable.

But when you've begun shopping and can't find anything you really like (and you've invested too much time and money into the project now to buy anything you don't like) for less than $80, you're suddenly $360 over the dollar amount in the budget. But you're not done yet. Wait until the electrician shows up with the bulbs. These are both mandatory and an extra cost. Halogen and low voltage bulbs can cost several times the amount of a standard 60 watt bulb. Multiply an extra $5 per bulb by twelve (fixtures) and you've increased the lighting allowance by $60, ballooning your line item by more than 50%!

By the time lighting selections are complete, the uninformed owner has usually taken a couple of hits to the checkbook with some change orders and is peeved this project is costing more than he was told. Why, he wonders, weren't the dollars allotted for the allowance items more realistic and in line with the level of finish he wanted for the project?

Number one, low figures on allowance items make the bottom line look good. The contractor knows the owner probably hasn't done any shopping for these items and is out of touch with pricing. Otherwise, they would be defined in the contract. This is the unhappy result of another decision put off until later by the homeowner.

Number two, the owner has been crying about spending dollars through the entire bidding process. The contractor also views allowance items as an opportunity for the homeowner to scrimp dollars on their own. The contractor can only save pennies on the cost of a 2x4 stud, for example, but the owner can generate real savings by selecting fixtures and finishes that are as plain as plain can be.

Plumbing fixtures, tile, carpet, and other unspecified finishes are usually allowances and can be a trap for the unwary consumer and provide sticker shock at the end of the job. While the contractor is obligated to keep clients apprised of change orders, he is usually under no obligation to make the client aware of allowance overages unless specified in the contract. Homeowners are free to spend as little or as much as they want. Smart homeowners selecting allowance items should compare the cost of their selections with the dollar amount in the budget. Brilliant homeowners will make their selections before the project begins.

Incomplete plans also skew the budget, generating change orders. Scrupulous contractors help the architect or designer flesh the plans out and attempt to bid all of the work required to complete the job. But that furnace flue that runs through the middle of the house and out the roof doesn't really enhance the design the architect has worked on for so long, so he conveniently forgets about it and leaves it off the plans. The unscrupulous contractor knows it needs to be moved and incorporated into the design at great expense, but only bids what is on the plans. For his own insurance he has a clause in his contract requiring the owner to pay for items not on the plans that are necessary to bring the project to completion. They will become change orders and their cost will be billed at an additional 25%. Another few thousand dollars at this point will make his bid too high and he's afraid he then won't get the job. It's better for him to wait until the project is underway and he can write up a change order and make an extra 25% on the architect's oversight.

Then the owner wants to know why the furnace flue wasn't on the plans. Soon enough, everyone is pointing fingers at everyone else and the teamwork required to bring a project to completion starts to dissolve in squabbles over professionalism (or lack of it) and dollars and cents.

Finally, most problems and complaints are generated because of disputes about the quality of the work or the level of finish.

Obviously, a contractor who performs substandard work that flunks the building department's criteria or is unacceptable to the architect and/or owner should not be paid until the problem is corrected. But let's be clear about what kind of "problem" needs to be corrected to justify withholding payment.

If an electrician or plumber "rough-ins" a project and their work doesn't pass the building department's inspection, then payment should be withheld until the violations are corrected and the building department signs off.

If the carpenter has hung ten doors and one door opens in the middle of the night, withholding 90% of the payment is appropriate, not the entire amount. If the door continues to open after a couple of return trips, maybe it's time to call a ghost buster.

If the final coat on a floor finish has footprints and dust that the contractor is responsible for, then final payment should be withheld until the floor is re-sanded and re-coated. If the old blind dog got up from a nap in the closet and padded across the wet floor, the owner should pay for the additional coat.

If the drywaller did a perfect job on the walls but left texture and mud all over the house, a certain portion of the payment *should* be withheld until the floors are cleaned up. But now it's time to digress.

If I want my floors cleaned, I call a cleaning person, hire a laborer I can supervise, or I do it myself. With all due respects to drywallers, they would be around the bottom of the list of floor-cleaning candidates. In an instance like this, the drywaller would be backcharged for the time and expense required to correct their mess. Before backcharging a contractor or subcontractor, however, they should receive a verbal or written notice stating the reason for the backcharge, the dollar amount involved, and a clear time frame for them to correct the problem using their own resources. (In this example, maybe the drywaller can hire a clean-up person.) The amount of the backcharge would equal the cost to correct the problem and possibly a percentage for administration fees.

If the architect inspects a cabinet installation and the drawers fall off the tracks and the doors are crooked, payment should be withheld until the problems are corrected.

Once in a while switches wind up on the wrong side of a door, the door's "swing" having changed during the course of the job sometime after the electrical was roughed in. Or, deciding on a kitchen floor after cabinets are installed can create a clearance problem – too much underlayment reduces critical height requirements for dishwashers and refrigerators.

But these are easy black and white examples. Most disputes are shaded with gray: If the upper cabinet doors bang into a light fixture too close to the cabinets, or new kitchen drawers hit appliance handles when they're pulled open, it may be in everyone's best interest to negotiate a dollars and cents compromise, if possible, rather than redoing the entire kitchen. Sometimes it makes sense to do some of the work and also knock dollars off the final price.

The contract should have specific guidelines for resolving complaints if the disputes cannot be resolved on an informal basis.

Remember Pat C___? The contractor replaced a steel column on his job because Pat thought it needlessly intruded into his new addition. The changes were made for aesthetic reasons only.

We built a two story addition on Pat's house. The upper level was the focal point of the project. The addition was built against his kitchen and living room. When the addition was closed in, the back wall was torn out and his new kitchen and new island overlooked the new "great room." It had a vaulted ceiling and corner picture windows on each end of the addition. The windows on the west framed one of the most famous mountains in the United States. The hardwood floor in the addition matched the existing floor perfectly. But there was one hitch.

At the end of the job Pat inspected everything very closely. He kept looking at the outside wall where the column stuck into the room a couple of months before. The walls were painted a light color and the floor was stained dark to match the existing floors; the contrast kept drawing his eye to an imperfection in the corner at the floor. The floor was not flat!

The existing floor of the old house was not level – it ran downhill from the old outside wall. There was a quarter-inch drop in about four feet. The new floor was dead-on level.

Pat didn't like the look of this – he wanted us to sand it flat.

Sanding a new floor was a dubious fix and liable to create more problems. I had already shaved the bottom of the baseboard to fit the angle of the floor. Even if the old floor ran downhill, the top of the base was level. I had done all that could be reasonably done. The fact that his existing floor was responsible for the problem didn't faze him. He was looking for a negotiating tool to knock some dollars off the final bill.

Then I reminded Pat that if we had left the column jutting into the room, the eye wouldn't have picked up the discrepancy. He seemed satisfied with this explanation, and a small side table in that spot effectively covered the problem.

The handiest weapon homeowners have against contractors who don't complete work or do inferior work is withholding payment until the project is completed satisfactorily. As soon as the contractor is ahead on the project dollars and cents-wise, some homeowners feel they are in danger of being behind the eight ball if the contractor is unscrupulous.

Many owners, especially women, tend to wrap other issues into a legitimate business dispute. While it is proper to withhold payment for a door installation if the door doesn't close, some clients may turn into "slow pays" because the carpenter has an annoying personality or made fun of their cat or their car.

Deal with the problem – don't get sidetracked on other issues.

Whatever the reasons for withholding payment, try to consider this – would a judge in a court of law agree or disagree with your position? And can you back it up?

Ron B___, the Grand Prize Award winner in the Contractors from Hell category, routinely bullied clients when his jobs turned south. Upset homeowners claimed he was bilingual, being fluent in English and profanity. According to victim interviews and files from the District Attorney's Consumer Fraud Division, this southerly change of direction always occurred after the first few days of work. In every case associated with Ron B___ and other contractors of his ilk, owners expressed deep regret that they caved in to his belligerence.

He rarely completed jobs. He strung out most of his victims with a litany of excuses and an M.O. of slow work habits, always ensuring he was on the upside of the job in a strictly dollars and cents basis. Over a couple of weeks, bad feelings would always simmer between contractor and victim. When the situation reached a critical mass because of continuing problems, these unwitting consumers often paid for shoddy work because they were worn down and bullied. One woman told him she would keep his equipment locked up until he returned money for uncompleted work. His response – he "would call the police." She felt threatened by the evil bugger and returned his equipment. He also invoked the name of his lawyer on a steady basis during the critical mass stage, as if this meant anything of substance.

Contractors from Hell curse and threaten homeowners if they balk at final payment, invoking their contract and sometimes threatening to call the police. The irony is, the homeowners should take them up on their threats because the last thing these small-time hoods really want is to see the authorities show up at the door.

Unsuspecting homeowners get worn down by the problems bad contractors cause. They eventually roll over – pay for bad work, or reach the point where they would rather deal with left-over problems and incomplete work by themselves rather than hold the contractor's feet to the fire.

Homeowners hoping to anticipate problems will recognize the tactics employed by these home-wreckers who lack all integrity and scruples.

Many homeowners have heard there will be a "little dust" during the course of a renovation. The contractor tells them to expect it.

But what they really said was, "The dust is little." Drywall dust is so small it has the ability to penetrate sheets of protective plastic, steel walls, finished flooring, and any and all barriers. (The same is true of wood dust generated by floor finishers.) I have convinced some drywallers that it enters the time-space continuum through tiny worm-holes to emerge in the opposite end of the house, desperately seeking a surface to settle on. The rest think I'm loco.

Regardless of the physics involved, wise homeowners will figure in extra cleaning time and expense above and beyond what the contractor calls for. Before the project begins, it's a good idea to discuss with the contractor exactly what level of cleanliness you expect during the course of the job.

And the little dust? That was just mis-communication.

The one simplest way to avoid most problems is to communicate, communicate, and communicate with all of the concerned parties.

Small problems turn into big problems when there is no communication. This basic law of the universe is amplified tenfold during the course of a construction project.

Communication is vital. Homeowners must be allowed to ask "stupid" questions of their contractors. Remember, no questions are stupid.

Being uninformed is stupid.

The home improvement industry generates more gripes, over time, than any other field. Consumers are initially aggravated when contractors don't return calls and pages. If a homeowner looking for a contractor hasn't had their calls returned after a reasonable period of time, they can logically assume that the contractor is out of town, is deathly ill, has gone out of business, is too swamped with immediate issues to contact a new client, or is blowing you off. In many instances, the answer is a combination of these. If you are a homeowner and searching for a contractor, do you really want to hire someone you can't get a hold of? In a case like this, follow the contractor's lead and get someone else.

It is imperative to keep lines of communication open, and not let personalities get in the way of problem-solving. Frequent meetings, whether on a daily or weekly basis, (depending on the length of the project), are always appropriate. The owner that is tuned in to the intricacies and zaniness of the remodeling process will have a better understanding of the necessities required to keep the project on course.

If the project has run aground and is hopelessly mired in one or more disputes, expect the owner and contractor to do everything required to protect their interests. Unwise owners and contractors will become emotional and belligerent. Owners should realize that whining will not serve their best interests.

Contractors have a leg up on homeowners when a project reaches this nadir because of their experience dealing with complaints and problems. They know most homeowners are remodeling novices and don't know how to complain. Smart homeowners need to be informed and need to know how to handle complaints.

Wrong way: I was framing a basement when the owner stormed downstairs in the morning and pointed out a gooey gloppy wad of amber sap oozing from a knot-hole in a 2x4. "Your boss is ripping us off by using green lumber in our house!" she screamed in my face. "When is he getting here? I'm not going to stand for this!"

In the first place, the 2x4 was perfectly kiln-dried lumber. It only had an "offending" knot. Lots of boards have lots of knots – this woman only advertised her ignorance. Secondly, she should have brought this issue up with my boss, not the powerless peon that was me. Thirdly, she was way too emotional about a stupid knot. Obviously, I was ignorant of other issues.

There are certain rules of decorum to follow that will help your complaint receive the proper attention.

Correct way to handle serious complaints: Be precise about the problem and put it in writing. "The closet doors in the east bedroom are trimmed too short. The bottoms are three inches above the carpet. They should only be one inch above the carpet."

Know what you want. "We want the doors to be replaced with new doors that are trimmed to the correct height, which is just under an inch of clearance between the bottom of the door and the top of the carpet. This involves staining and finishing the new doors and reinstalling the hardware."

Set a reasonable time frame for the work to be done. "We know these doors take a week to be delivered, and the painter and carpenter need to be scheduled in. We expect the doors will be replaced within 30 calender days from the date of this letter." Not, "Before my sister starts her new job," or "When the kids get out of school." Otherwise, they'll be done, "When the mortgage is paid off."

Be sure to include the date and your phone number. Make a follow-up call to the builder a few days later to make sure they received the letter. In the initial stages of "the problem," communicate directly with the builder. Don't complain to his lawyer, banker, the building department, any government agencies, subcontractors, or the peon banging boards together in the basement. This only alienates the contractor and he will be less likely to schedule in corrections. Good contractors want to take care of problems – the assumption is you've hired a good contractor already. Now, give him the opportunity to correct the problem.

Impossible homeowners waste time picking every little detail to death during construction. Wait until the job is complete before passing judgment on most items. Chances are, the contractor already knows about most of the little goof-ups and has them on the sub's list when they return for a final time.

Lots of problems and issues do surface at the end of the job after the project is over. (See "Finished!!") Look there for final solutions.

Unfortunately, little problems can snowball during the course of the job. The best strategy is tackling them as they turn up to avoid being blind-sided at the end.

The joy of remodeling is that each job is different. The pain in the butt of remodeling is that each job is different. No two houses and/or clients will be the same. Just as many homeowners can't visualize their blueprints in 3-D, builders don't have X-ray vision. Consequently, the contractor can only guess about problems behind the walls.

The X-Factor. Imagine three scrupulous contractors bidding work on your home. The first contractor bids only the work requested. He is inexperienced and his bid may be too low. The second contractor knows more work is involved to achieve the homeowner's objective, and bids accordingly. His price is naturally higher. The third contractor is savvy and knows there is a wide price range for a job like this. His tactic is common – bid a lot of work and bid it high. (This is fine if he can back up his price with performance and quality.) He knows he can get away with this because there is often a wide gulf between the low and high bid. The trouble is, the bid may be wildly high if he assumes the worst.

There are ways to mitigate the X-factor.

If there actually are serious problems behind the walls, the owner should logically know this before the framers arrive. When a major project is in the design phase, homeowners and architects should consider paying a contractor to investigate the structure. Call it exploratory surgery. Lift up a section of flooring to see what's underneath, check how many layers of shingles are on the roof, and open up and patch holes in the walls to eliminate as many surprises as possible.

Some jurisdictions require soils tests before digging out for an addition. A backhoe cuts a hole a little deeper than the projected excavation, and a soils engineer peers down, inspects the soil visually and sends a sample to the lab. And on smaller projects, it might be prudent and economical to hire a laborer to dig out along the foundation wall before $100 an hour worth of heavy machinery rumbles into the yard and then has to stop everything but the proverbial meter while decisions are being made in the field.

The high cost of labor makes unforeseen delays increasingly expensive. Design/build contracts on major remodels make sense to many owners.

Projects today are getting increasingly complicated; the design process can be long and arduous. It can take a year between the time a new kitchen is decided on and the old cabinets are emptied.

Good planning is as essential as good communication to mitigate problems. Homeowners and architects can help their own causes by doing a records check with the local building department to learn what work was done to the structure in the past. Also, there may be old plans on file that may answer questions that pop up during the design process.

Santa Clauses happen, but you don't have to be a Grinch to uncover them beforehand.

Psychotic Remodeling

RICK'S
TIPS

SAVVY SUPERS photograph everything during the construction process – underground pipes, drains, and cables; anything and everything that will be buried underground. A thorough photographic record should also be taken after framing inspections are complete. Insulators and dry-wallers "bury" about one in thirty electrical boxes. A photographic record shows exactly where water piping lies in the walls, which is indispensable knowledge to a trim carpenter ready to poke holes in a bathroom wall to mount hardware.

FROM THE BUILDING WITH CAULK DEPARTMENT. Use uninsulated 14 gauge copper wire to puncture the caulk tube below the nozzle when a thin bead is required. Electricians leave it all over the job before they finish their rough-in – snag a few short lengths and stash them in your toolbox.

Electricians also leave "twist-locks" around. Used for locking wires together, the red ones make perfect caps for opened caulk tubes.

Also, carve the tube's nozzle with a knife to create a right angle on the tip for a perfect bead in an imperfect corner. Keep lacquer thinner handy in a small plastic dish washing liquid bottle to squirt in the corners to smooth out excess silicone caulk.

EMERGENCY LIST. Cultivate a list of tradesmen to call before an emergency arises and you're left frantically thumbing through the phone book when the drains are backing up and your headed out the door to catch a flight. Ask friends and neighbors who they have used in the past and could recommend in the future. Then phone the business and ask if they do service work in your area, how much they charge for repairs, and ask if they have an emergency number that you can keep on file, just like fire, police, and hospital numbers. Ask if you can charge repairs if you're out of town.

Don't make an important decision in a panic.

DAILY REPORTS. Most remodeling contractors maintain daily logs on each project. These reports note daily attendance of workers and visitors, deliveries from suppliers, weather and temperature (thirteen inches of snow, gale-force winds), and chronicle decisions and problems. Their value is proved down the road if a dispute arises about "what happened when." Should that come to pass, don't depend on the contractor's word for it – maintain your own diary.

CREATE *reasonable* deadlines and try to hold contractors to them. "You will be back when ___? To do what___?" A sly follow-up/reminder call the day before lets them know you haven't forgotten a meeting, walk-thru, or the fact they're due back to repair or replace something.

LEAVE NOTES for the contractor or superintendent. This works both ways. It's not unusual for workers and owners to not see each other at all during the week, assuming everyone is working. A legal pad on the counter can pose questions for both sides – "Should the lights be centered between the beams or over the couch?" and *leave a written record of when decisions were made if the notes are dated.* Also, it usually provides time for both sides to reflect over needed decisions.

SIGN IN THE PAINT STORE: "Please bring us a sample to match, not a pigment of your imagination."

AMATEUR DRYWALLERS create lots of insidious dust when they have to sand a patch flat or a wall smooth. I remember hauling a couple of five gallon buckets full of drywall dust out of one of my earliest basements. Now I get a nice finish the smart way:

Scrape ridges and peaks flat with your taping knife, then wipe the drywall joints smooth with a big, warm sponge, being careful to not take off too much joint compound. Save the mesh sandpaper for inside corners at the ceilings or large humps, depending on the level of your drywall finishing skills.

NAILS AND SCREWS FOR TRIM AND DRYWALL. Are eight enough or is nine too many? Most codes require screws every twelve inches along the studs or ceiling joists and every eight inches in the corners.

There are no code guidelines for installing trim (like base and casing). But if it moves, it needs more fastening, period. Construction adhesive is a great product, especially for tiny pieces that would otherwise split.

WASPS AND HORNETS often make their homes in walls and under the eaves, and become especially riled when their homes get torn up, too. I always keep a can of spray glue, available at most office supply stores, in my nail bag when I have to work around ill-tempered yellowjackets. One squirt gums them up in an instant, and they drop to the ground in mid-flight. Spray glue is a lot safer and more effective than spraying chemical pesticides, especially if there are dogs, cats, birds, and little kids around the property.

Do-It-Yourselfers who discover a nest of these irritable striped demons on their property can execute their own hostile takeover during a night raid with this ultimate weapon: A can of triple expanding urethane foam. This spray foam, usually less than five bucks a can, is commonly used to seal drafts around piping penetrations, window frames, and other sources of air infiltration. One application sends a horrifying tsunami of gooey sticky gunk through the cells of their nests, and then expands over the course of a few hours, gobbling up and permanently entombing the little buggers.

Most cans have a convenient flexible spray tube that attaches to the nozzle. The tip is just about the size of the portal to a yellowjacket home. Insert this into the narrow fissure the wasps have been exiting and entering all day. The best time is late at night, when most of them are nesting for the evening, or late on a cool day when they are least active.

STEALING SAVES TIME AND MONEY. Color selections are an inexact science to most homeowners. It's not uncommon for homeowners to repaint walls or siding two or more times to achieve the color and hue they originally envisioned. I look at previously painted homes and projects for colors that "work."

When I'm working in a home that considerable thought and planning has gone into, and the color scheme is impressive, I'll put some paint aside and save it for future use. When it was time to repaint the exterior of our home, my wife knocked on the door of a house whose colors we admired and asked the homeowner where the paint came from. Though somewhat startled, the owner took the question as a compliment and gave us the exact colors.

Study sources that experts have put a lot of time and thought into. Training and experience are very useful when selecting colors for a palette as large as a house. Steal colors and schemes if you like them. (Most are not copyrighted.) Tour show homes, and pay attention to ads. One client even matched the kitchen colors of the set of her favorite TV sitcom!

PET PEEVE: Misaligned electrical boxes. When electricians set their boxes for switches and outlets, they usually just measure up from the floor. But old homes often have out-of-level floors. Some trades are unaffected by this condition (painters, carpet layers, roofers.) But cabinets and tile must be run level or they just don't fit together.

Boxes for outlets above the kitchen counter must be run level, not measured off the floor. And they must be measured from the highest point of the floor, since base cabinets will be shimmed up from the lowest point.

Backsplashes above kitchen counters require particular attention. Boxes must clear preformed, laminate backsplashes. If the backsplashes are tile, the homeowner or superintendent should communicate to the electrician the placement of the boxes so they will fit into the tile design instead of collide with it. In a perfect installation, level grout lines will consistently line up with every box. A variation of more than an eighth of an inch separates a great job from a mediocre one.

Tile patterns and the Electrical Code also impact box placement. Whoever is responsible for backsplash (and kitchen) design should be familiar with both.

SIDEBAR: There is an almost infinite variety of materials, textures, and colors for kitchen backsplashes. Selections are more limited for electrical devices and cover plates. This is why homeowners sometimes frown when they see a twenty five cent plastic ivory cover plate centered in the middle of their twenty-five hundred dollar Mephisto Mauve Swirl granite backsplash. For granite and marble backsplashes, faux painters have moved into the market by creating plate covers that are camouflaged against the stone.

FLOOR TRACKS. Until remodelers start packing levitators in their tool boxes, it is nearly impossible to roll a large object over a newly finished floor without carving tracks in the finish. If your kitchen is the new home of a 500 lb. refrigerator, or a piano goes back into the newly refinished front room, always schedule a final coat of floor finish **after** the heavy lifting is over.

Man, agitated by washer, fires 3 shots into machine

Associated Press

CHIPPEWA FALLS, Wis. — A man who pushed his washing machine down the stairs and then shot it was quoted by investigators as saying he was angry with the appliance.

Guy Boos, 37, pushed the washer down the stairs from the second floor and onto a driveway beside a garage, then fired three shots with a .25-caliber pistol from about 40 feet, police said.

He was arrested because he discharged a weapon within 100 feet of a dwelling, they said. Boos was booked by police Wednesday on allegations that he endangered safety. He has not been formally charged by the district attorney's office.

IT'S A GOOD THING this enraged homeowner didn't have to call a plumber. Rick's tip – next time, take the thing for a long ride to an empty lot before plugging it – just like the pros in the mob.

OVERSPRAY. Painters shake their heads when asked about this taboo topic, acting as if it occurs as often as a fifty year flood. But remember that overexposure to toxic fumes contributes to short-term memory loss and overspray from their painting rigs can cause more damage than the original cost of many jobs. Ask the painter if he puts a heavy tarp on the roof before he sprays the gutters and fascia, and make sure cars are garaged or parked around the corner before your house is sprayed. **It is**

almost impossible to get paint off shingles and cars. Good spots to find minor bits of overspray are on door hinges and around windows.

Remember, many good painters spend as much time masking off a job as they do painting it!

DROP CLOTHS are essential tools for remodelers. Their disadvantages are that they move around a lot and tend to collect dust. Even modest spills will soak right through. I've been using scrap sheet vinyl for years when operating in someone's home. They store easily, make great runners, protect existing floors, and are easy to clean and sweep.

GARBAGE DISPOSALS. Here's an old plumber's trick for freeing jammed disposals: (After making sure the power is off) jam a broomstick against the flat wheel that is just beneath the whirly-gig cutting blades. Exerting steady and even pressure, push the disc until it spins freely. Small staples, bones, and fibrous veggies tend to collect along the sides of the wheel. Push the reset button on the bottom of the unit if necessary.

To sweeten your disposer's breath and keep it clean, chop up a lemon and toss it down the hatch every now and then.

NAVAL JELLY is a good lube for light bulb bases. Anal retentive homeowners can apply a dose to the bulb base before screwing it into the socket. That, and matching the wattage of the bulb to what's listed on the fixture will practically eliminate twisting light bulbs in half when they're being changed.

HOME INSPECTORS. Unless you're a long-time pro in the home-improvement field, hiring a good house inspector before making the purchase of a lifetime is absolutely necessary. Your home inspector should walk the roof, crawl beneath the house, and check the attic...

Charlie and Rulisa M___, of Little Rock, Arkansas, had been remodeling an 85 year-old home for two years when the terrible thing happened. They told the *Arkansas Democrat-Gazette* that they had an eerie feeling the whole time they lived in their house. When Charlie pulled down the ceiling on the top floor one day, a headless skeleton fell from the attic. Police speculated the poor creature had been up there for decades. Rulisa told the newspaper, "I don't have any theories about who it might be, but I do know that it has been trying to lead us to it ever since we got here."

15

HOMEOWNERS FROM HELL

I have never met a homeowner directly from Hell, but I can recall a few who were headed in that direction.

Pat R___ and I first met in the lobby of her newly acquired luxury high rise condo, set in the heart of downtown's historic district. Pat explained that she sold real estate, and my initial impression of this smartly dressed woman in her mid fifties was that she was a savvy businesswoman with the financial and mental wherewithal to be a good client. Pat wanted this project on the fast track, i.e., design as you build. I was comfortable with that as long as the homeowner was experienced and knew what was involved. She wanted to move on this project quickly. Pat was a better talker than she was a businesswoman, but I didn't realize at the time by how much.

She wore a long camel-colored overcoat, minced through the lobby in three inch heels, and wore a little too much base over her boozer's nose. She had gotten my name as a referral. She didn't tell me who the client was, and I never pursued her about it. In retrospect, I should have pinned her down. I had been renovating a number of condos recently, and I thought we would be a good fit. I actually looked forward to working with her. We rode the elevator to the eighth floor and she began to tell me her plans. A couple of walls were going, and she wanted new cabinets, countertops, fixtures, and appliances; repaint and re-carpet. Update the lighting. It was a standard remodel, and a nice one to snag a month before Christmas.

We first met in mid-November, and Pat stressed how anxious she was to get the project underway. I had been talking to a couple of other clients who were hemming and hawing, and I was getting frustrated with them. I had a feeling they would put off their projects until next year, leaving me in the lurch at Christmas time. Most people don't want an army of construction workers in their home in December, and who can blame them? I wouldn't either. Consequently, this unlived-in condo would make the perfect home for my holiday. I pounced on it like a panther.

Less than a week later I had a set of plans for the building department in one hand and a signed contract in the other. Although the new floor plan and electrical scheme was fixed, Pat had not made any selections yet for her interior finish. She was due to meet her decorator on the job next week, and the logical assumption was that most of the required decisions would be made then. Fine.

I was in daily communication with Pat, updating her on the status of the permit. Thursday morning I told her the permit had been issued; I would pick it up later in the day, post it on the job site, and move tools up to the eighth floor on Friday. Demolition would begin on Monday morning.

Pat was fairly insistent I begin demolition on Friday. It didn't take much lobbying on her behalf for me to agree with her, so Friday afternoon we got a lot of the demo underway. We ripped up all the carpet and padding and set it on the balcony. It was in good condition, but the new floor plan would render it useless. (I actually got a little cash for it at the salvaged carpet yard, which was certainly a better deal than paying to dump it.) All of the outdated fixtures were removed from the walls and ceilings and piled in one corner of the back bedroom. The wall separating the kitchen from the dining area was a casualty of that first day. We took out half of the kitchen cabinets, the oven, and began a good-sized pile of wall rubble. The partition walls were heavy metal framing with two layers of drywall on each side, and enough metal lath mixed into the equation to make demolition tedious. But we had plenty of saw blades, and really felt like giving it hell that day, so we were able to get most of the master bedroom wall demolished and on the rubble pile before wrapping it up for the weekend.

I left a message with Pat Saturday morning to update her on our progress. We had gotten a lot accomplished on Friday, and I felt really good about the job until I received a call from Pat Sunday night. She was in a terrible panic.

Unfortunately, Pat had not been entirely candid with me. It turned out she had not closed on the property. Her financing had not gone through, but she had expected it would happen any day. She babbled on about how she filed as a self employed real estate agent, had claimed lots of deductions that reduced her income, and couldn't qualify for a loan at the rate she wanted. In the dollars and cents world of the mortgage company she was presently screwed. It turned out she got a key through her real estate office, not from the owner. But this wasn't the bad news.

The bad news was, the listing agent decided to check on the property over the weekend. He wanted to make sure it was in good condition. There was, after all, a contract on it.

Was he surprised!

I'm sure he looked at the damage in stunned silence, wandering through piles of rubble, avoiding the electrical conduit and outlet boxes dangling from the ceiling and poking through the bare concrete floor. Pat R___ knew the actual owners lived in Hawaii and she believed she would close way before anyone found out she ordered the place demolished. The listing agent phoned the owners late Saturday morning. They flew three thousand miles to survey the damage, and had a powwow with their lawyer and broker Sunday afternoon before threatening to sue Pat.

I was furious also. Besides having represented Pat as the *owner* of a property with the City and County, my work ground to a halt while this mess was sorted out. Pat made one thing clear: I wouldn't be on the hook for the damage. I of course knew that, but I was relieved she was willing to take responsibility for the whole mess. Pat vowed to get it straightened out, then cited the case of Bill___, a local attorney she knew who gutted a recently purchased town home before closing and without the benefit of a building permit. I had never heard of Bill___'s town home, but I sure knew Bill___.

My former partner, Larry F___, and I had finished Bill___'s home eighteen months earlier. Bill was a legal bully who did whatever he wanted and then waited for people to sue him if they didn't like it. Neat guy. Larry dealt with Bill 99% of the time. I never liked him and directed my energies to getting the work completed and ironing out his issues with the building department. But Bill paid his bills on time and we had a nice job in a great location.

Bill's house was a brick and stone Tudor mansion on a tree-lined avenue with a parkway just up the street from the City Park, Museum, and the Zoo. Built in the 1920's, the interior was terrazzo and wrought-iron, with walls paneled in mahogany. It was a beautiful home in a high-profile area.

Bill was only replacing the old garage, so he figured, "Why bother with a permit? If the building department wants to make a big deal out of it, I'll just sort it out with them later."

But the new garage was right on the property line, and provided access to the existing house, which didn't sit too well with the zoning department. The new garage had room for two BMW's and a complete wood shop any carpenter would die for but no carpenter could afford. It had commercial planers, table saws, a radial arm saw, a shaper, and a dust collection system. Bill agonized over the placement of each and every tool and overhead light. He always wanted a wood shop, and thought he might get motivated to learn how to use the equipment now that it was handy. The entire garage required as much electricity as a small village in Mexico, and Bill had to pull in additional power from the pole in the alley. The new garage had a downstairs with a sauna, shower, and weight room that was convenient after using the backyard pool and provided a secondary entrance to the existing house.

The new garage had a red tag from the building department, closing the project down until Bill got his permits in order.

Bill___ was acting as his own general contractor when he started the project. It was out of the ground and the ceiling joists were rolled when we showed up. One of the subs knew Larry, so when the job shut down the sub gave Bill our number to bail him out.

Then I knew where Pat had gotten my name.

I was also furious with Pat because I had committed so much time and energy to this particular project, and I had nothing else going on if this fell through. I was determined to not let this Grinch steal Christmas, so I tried to make the best of a bad situation. If this job was a fish, I would have thrown it back.

Pat eventually closed on her loan in about a week, paid a higher rate, paid damages to the previous owners, and paid for their air fare and lodging. I thought my troubles were over, but they were just beginning.

She was very apologetic for the fiasco she created, and I was anxious to get this show on the road. She arranged a meeting with the designer, Holly H___, and the three of us met in what was left of the kitchen to try and pick up the pieces.

I walked Holly through the project, and then we talked about what decisions needed to be made. Doors, countertops, and carpet needed to be ordered. Sinks and hardware and faucets and shower doors needed to be selected. At the end of the meeting there was an extensive list, but I knew a couple of days of serious thought should whittle it down to a few items. I wasn't worried.

Then Pat announced she was going to the coast for three weeks to be with her boyfriend. The stress was starting to get to her. Holly was left with the decisions. Fine.

The next day I got the project rolling again, continuing the demolition and trying to get some answers out of Holly. She confessed to me she had never met Pat until the day of our meeting and had no idea what Pat's tastes were. She was as shocked as I was when Pat announced she was leaving.

(This is *not* fiction. "Pat" is not a composite of my ten worst clients.)

In all honesty, Holly wasn't much of a decorator. She had trouble with decisions. If she was on the Titanic she probably couldn't decide which lifeboat to get in. The fact that she was a half-way quality human being, however, made Pat suffer by comparison. Holly was reluctant to make any decisions on her own, even though she was acting as the homeowner's agent in this situation. She wanted to tinker with the floor plan a little. In my opinion, the original design was not great but it was "OK," and that it was too late to start making wholesale changes. Moving walls would hold up everything. Besides, how much can be done with a 600 square foot apartment? We were eliminating one bedroom and adding space to the master and expanding the closet. Holly's proposals, to my mind, were minor and would only cause more delays. I needed decorating decisions, not headaches. The last thing I was going to do was change *anything* on this job without a signed change order. So we got as far as we could, and wrote up half a dozen change orders for Pat to sign when she got back.

This was the BF era (Before Faxes), so it was difficult to keep Pat up to date on the design process while she was out of town. When she returned she expected to see drywall completed. Instead, she arrived to a fistful of change orders and a partially drywalled apartment. She was furious the drywall wasn't done, but after I reminded her of the change order process and pointed out the line in the contract stating no changes shall be made without written authorization. She settled down a bit and exclaimed she had no idea she needed to sign these things. She was going to have her boyfriend (a heating contractor) review them and then sign them off. The changes concerned door style (Holly wanted a two-panel door that was not available), moving one small wall a couple of feet, widening the opening to the master, and relocating the stereo built-ins. Most of these changes impacted the electrical work – switches, outlets, phone lines and lights would all change from the original plan.

The final change order was for the electrical work. Pat disappeared for a couple of days (I guess she went on a binge) and returned with a couple of the less critical change orders signed. Other change orders, that were more of a design issue, (like rerouting cold-air returns and extending soffits, even eliminating the breakfast bar,) she signed and then scrawled across the bottom things like, "looking at other options," and "not doing," all evidence of a brain that was badly misfiring. Then she left for the coast again, the job sputtered along, and she returned with her boyfriend, who walked through the job and thought everything looked good. This seemed to cheer her up a bit, and I worked with "Dick," who had a refreshing no-nonsense nuts and bolts approach to the project. Then the job sat while we waited for Holly's doors to arrive, and then we hit the Christmas/New Year's slump. The holidays fell on Wednesdays, no work was allowed in the building on weekends, and six days work was accomplished in two weeks time.

All of the loose ends were wrapped up by mid-January, and it was time to settle the bill. Pat had the audacity to blame me for the delays. Her smarmy boyfriend, "Dick," knew better but sat by her side like an inert blob while she pulled out her list of supposed wrongs, indignities, and financial hardships.

They were all bogus. She wanted me to pay her mortgage for a month because the job ran over, reimburse her for an old washer/dryer combo she told me to give away at the beginning of the job (a Salvation Army receipt wasn't good enough) and pay the interest on her loan. I went through the roof. We eventually settled that afternoon, mainly because I *had* to get money that day to pay the electrician, trim supplier, and personal bills. I signed a waiver against any future claims – the dollar amount I was stiffed for was about $1,500. I've always regretted doing that, but the advantage was I would never have to see or deal with that woman ever again. In that respect, I got off cheap.

Pat R___ was a bad homeowner for a number of reasons. She failed to accept any responsibility for her actions, failed to make critical decisions in a timely manner, failed to sign change orders on a timely basis, and failed to communicate her tastes and desires to her designated agent and advocate, the designer.

I was at fault because I should have had a clause in the contract that said something like this: "Each day a decision is past due, the scheduled completion date shall automatically be extended by an equal amount." Of course, there was no scheduled completion date at all, only a verbal guesstimate, which is not binding.

Had there been a penalty clause for missing a deadline written into the contract, the dollar amount is usually clearly stated – whether it is $25 or $100 a day. Under such a contract, change orders usually buy more time. Before the job began I handed her a blank change order and asked if she knew how they affected the contract and the job. She assured me she was quite familiar with them. This one was on the "fast track," after all, and the job would be full of them. I guess if I had listened to some of my instincts, I might have guessed where that track was headed.

The true testament to her eventual destination, however, was her lack of integrity at the beginning of the project, when she actually lied about owning the place and then couldn't wait for me to demolish a place that wasn't hers.

Although Pat never delayed payments during the course of the job, clients who don't pay or are slow pays will top any contractor's list of slimeball homeowners.

The "slow pays" promise to write out that $3,000 check after someone drives out and cleans up 30 cents worth of screws they found in the gutter. The anxious contractor drives out with an extension ladder, can't find any screws in the gutter, and then can't find anyone home to cut a check that was promised. Follow-up phone calls don't get returned. Experienced contractors can usually spot the "slow pays" before the job is over – they are always complaining about little things. Many "slow pays" are so worried they are going to get screwed that they feel their only defense is to pay late. (The others flat out don't have the cash and can't meet their legal commitments.) They refuse to believe they might have hired a good contractor that will return to fix any mistakes. Instead, they act as though they are waiting for mistakes to happen, and then plan to adjust the final payment accordingly over the next few months.

Logically, "no pays" are worse than "slow pays." They don't answer their phones after bills are due, and are not scared by the threat of a lien. Adding in attorney's fees, loss of work time, and court costs, they know it isn't always profitable for contractors to seek justice. But contractors who have been burned once too often, just like many homeowners, soon reach the point where they don't care what it costs to recover funds. In a perfect world, "no pays" would only hire "Contractors from Hell."

There are more books, articles, pamphlets and web-sites that provide homeowners with information on how to select a contractor than one owner could ever use. But homeowners need to know contractors look for certain qualities in an owner, and it's in the homeowner's best interest to exhibit those qualities.

I like to size up my clients – one way I avoid problems is to not bid every job that comes down the pike. This is fine when the local economy is good, and business isn't slow. If I'm in the middle of a walk-thru of a small project and realize I don't want to have any business dealings with these people because: a) the job is a nightmare b) they strike me as smarmy c) I feel they're financially challenged for the work they're considering, I tell them I can't get around to it for several months. If they say that's OK, we're in no hurry, I mail them an estimate that I have given little thought to, except for the dollar amount, which is ridiculously high. Thankfully, I haven't reached the stage where I walk into someone's home and tell them I don't want to have to have anything to do with them.

Contractors like to work for homeowners who know what they want. This means owners have to do their homework. Clip a picture out a magazine showing the contractor what you like and why you like it. Owners who show me photos of the entry to their friend's house, or suggest I look at the front porch two blocks away, have told me they know what they want and know how to communicate it. Even if talking to a contractor is the first step in their "small" remodel, being able to communicate what they want is a big first step.

I can't tell you how many times I've wandered aimlessly through all sizes of houses with owners intent on providing home tours but reluctant to provide any pertinent information about goals or budget. At the end of a walk-thru like that, I have six pages of notes about what works and what doesn't, but no sense of priorities, no budget, or no concrete idea of what the owner really wants to have a bid on. There is some value in getting acquainted with a prospective client, but there is a lot more to be said for a productive walk-thru. Contractors are usually busy people with ten irons in the fire at once. They are not necessarily mind readers.

Consultants advise remodelers to look for the following qualities in their relationships with a prospective client:

Trust. Has the contractor, during the initial meeting process, earned the homeowner's trust? If the contractor is constantly being second guessed by the owner, the answer is probably "no."

Advice. Does the homeowner take the contractor's advice?

Control. Is the homeowner willing to allow the contractor to control the job once it is underway?

Communication. Does the client communicate their ideas and desires to the contractor? And if the remodeler is dealing with a couple, does the couple communicate with each other and not disagree about major issues and/or design details?

If the answer is "No" to any of these questions, remodelers are advised to either reverse the client's thinking or ditch the job.

Contractors like to work for clients who can make up their minds. Homeowners who vacillate continually about whether they are really going to do a job or not soon lose most contractor's interest if no progress is made and a sincere effort is made on the contractor's part to nudge the homeowner along. Good contractors are busy contractors. They don't have time to hold the hand of every homeowner who is "thinking about (fill in the blank) to their house" and doesn't make a serious effort to figure out what they really want. Homeowners like this are fairly common and *we can recognize you at the conclusion of the second visit to your home*. It's not whether the door should be on the east side or the west side? that tips us off, it's that you're clearly unwilling to make an emotional and dollars and cents commitment to planning and scheduling the work. "Mother of Mary," the contractor thinks to himself, "If they can't decide if they want to even do the work, what will happen when they've got a three page list of critical decisions in their hand?"

Homeowners undergoing a major remodel often need to make critical decisions on a daily basis. Problems arise when the homeowner is unused to making decisions ("Do you want six pound or eight pound padding, Maam? I gotta know now.") beyond whether she should use Hamburger Helper Tuna or Chicken?

Pet peeve: Homeowners who call to have me bid on an addition. The next day I'm standing in their back yard and I learn by asking twenty questions they've given zero thought to the size or cost of the project. During a one hour conversation the project changes from a family room/study to a guest suite. Then they hint they have some extra money they would like to invest in the house. When they tell me the dollar amount, I have to tell them that's not enough money to complete even the framing of the project, whatever it may turn out to be. Then they want me to price this nebulous concept that will never coalesce in their back yard. When this happens, I measure out an area the size of a couple of rooms for them and give them a rounded up square foot estimate. Then I tell them they'll have to pay someone to design a set of plans that the building department can review and contractors and subs alike can bid. The next move is theirs.

Homeowners looking for "free estimates" need to demonstrate to a contractor that they are serious about the project at hand. Too often, Homeowners from Hell confuse free estimates with free design services.

Homeowners intent on an excursion to that well-known place may rely on contractors to provide decorating guidelines. Don't ask a contractor what kind of drapes and carpeting he likes unless you expect him to move in after the job is completed. His job is to to create a world that suits the homeowner's taste and style. Everyone's taste is different and unique, and not necessarily interchangeable.

I remember doing three kitchens in sequence. The first was very modern and stark and had a distinct commercial feel, with lots of stainless steel, dark tile, exposed metal posts and wire brushed brick. The second was a very old-fashioned kitchen in an old-fashioned house – even the kitchen sink and drainboard came from a salvage yard. The kitchen looked state of the art when it was finished – but from the late 1940's. The final kitchen was straight out of a Big Box store. It had sleek oak cabinets, laminate countertops, a stainless steel sink, and a vinyl floor. Nothing unusual, but it was very nice and serviceable and fit in perfectly with the rest of the house. The point is, any one of the three owners would have retched if their kitchens looked like the other two. It's incumbent upon the homeowners to communicate as best they can their vision of the finished product, even in the early stages of the design process.

Homeowners who are confused about what might be right for their home should consider contacting an interior designer. They are licensed and trained in shaping the home environment to suit the personalities of the owner and accommodate the idiosyncrasies of the house. Contractors are a good resource for more practical matters. If we select this tile, will we need to add more sub-flooring? Are the existing joists adequate? If we add windows to this wall, what are the chances of us having to move wiring and plumbing? If we close off this window, can we find siding that matches? And what is the price range for this work? The very best contractors can help guide homeowners through these processes. They may even know the perfect architect or decorator, or have their own staff of design professionals that can translate the barest of ideas into a thing of stone and steel.

Homeowners looking for the right designer for their home can check with the local ASID (American Society of Interior Designers) for a referral. Homeowners should be able to explain the scope of their work (redecorate the entire house, no structural; remodel the bathrooms; or, main floor/addition, etc.) so the organization can best match the client with the designer, who make their money one of three ways: Charging an hourly rate; charging a percentage of what they sell to the homeowner (draperies, furniture, etc.); or any and all combinations of the above.

Oftentimes, I get some of my best work through designers. The good ones build strong relationships with potential clients, and have also established their own network of contractors and tradesmen who operate in the same work-world. "Decorators" also provide professional services, but the requirements to be a decorator are not as stringent as those required of a "Designer," which designers are always quick to point out to novice clients.

(There is a frustrating time in the design chronology when the plan bounces from the architect to the owner, from the designer to the contractor, and then around the horn a few more times in a random pattern. No real progress seems to be made. At this point, the plan is in the Bermuda Triangle. The architect is adding items and finishes the owner really doesn't want; the builder wants to see construction details on the plans instead; the owner could care less about these details, he's concerned about little incidental costs everyone is finding that have begun to add up. The plans just seem to drift around and not much seems to get accomplished. The Bermuda Triangle phase is a normal part of the process and is the time when all of the parties can advance their agenda and refine the plans.)

When the scope of work is well-defined, it's time to address the budget.

Homeowners from Hell will have no idea what the project costs and/or refuse to tell the contractor what they can afford to spend. In some cases they are afraid the contractor will simply rob them, driving the cost of the project above their budget. Actually, true professionals need to know that number so they can tailor the project to meet the budget. Reliable contractors know how to build to the budget. (Selecting a reliable contractor is the most important decision the owner will make in the remodel process.) Homeowners who are coy about the budget are leaving the contractor with one of two impressions: a) the client has recently received an inheritance from an oil sheik to live in a house like this and not care about how much they expect to spend. b) The owner is a total idiot. It is infuriating to design to an owner's grandiose scheme of custom cabinets and granite tops and commercial appliances for their new kitchen, when the reality is, all they can afford is particleboard veneer doors and an upgraded laminate. Contractors spend too much time reconciling Cadillac tastes with Yugo budgets.

Sometimes it's almost a relief to be the dreaded third or fourth bidder on a job. At least the homeowner has reached the point where he knows what he wants and is comparing apples to apples. The walk-thru is more like a drill than a meandering home tour.

Remember, bad contractors don't care what your budget is. They will "lowball" a homeowner to get the job, then ring up all the extras toward the end of the project.

I've remodeled for a number of multi-millionaires. They have a generous yet sensible budget for the project at hand. Obviously, they already like the location and style of their home or they wouldn't be directing trunk loads of cash into it. But they also know how much they can expect to spend on a new kitchen or addition or basement finish. They know beforehand if they may be putting more money into the home than they will recover if they have to sell. Most of us aren't multi-millionaires, but we all have to make budget decisions that can be realistically built to.

Homeowners who have done their homework during the initial design process already have some sense about what a project will cost by talking to salespeople, learning what tradesmen charge per hour, or, for larger projects, sitting down with an architect or designer. Current "idea" magazines are also a good source of price ranges. As the scope of the work becomes fairly well-defined, the price range for the work will begin to coalesce. Then, homeowners will get an inkling of whether the proposed work fits into their budget.

Homeowners who make decisions based solely on price are, obviously, interested in the cheapest job possible. They may even gain some emotional satisfaction by holding the cheapest contractor to his bid. But they should know that the guy who is losing money at the end of the job will cut corners to save money. The result – an inferior job. Inexperienced homeowners don't often realize how cheap, inferior work can actually lower the value of their home. Low bids often indicate inexperience on the contractor's part, since no contractor wants to actually undertake a difficult remodel project with a low profit margin. An experienced contractor's strategy is this: He wants to bid as many jobs as he can and bid them too high, and then have only enough time and resources to do only the highest-paying work. He can get away with this because there is usually a wide range of prices among the various bids on any single project. This wide range will shrink if the project has detailed plans and all of the fixtures, appliances, finishes, and work has been specified ("spec'd") by an experienced designer or architect hired by the homeowner. If the contractor can back up the high price with quality work and punctuality, fine.

If in doubt about who to hire for a major project, rely on the architect's advice about which contractor might be most appropriate for the project.

(Word of caution: Don't rely too heavily on an architect's opinion about costs, although expect them to provide useful dollars and cents guidelines. In all fairness, construction costs change too rapidly for architects to keep track of, and if cornered they will be the first ones to tell you estimating isn't their job. They are correct, but it's well-known in the industry that the majority of architects are out of touch with mundane areas like pricing and estimating. This is fine, unless you are requesting an architect to design to a budget, which is what many clients ask. Homeowners who believe architect's pricing are excellent candidates for "sticker shock."

There is a range of square foot costs for new homes, kitchen remodels, decks, basement finishes, and other projects that can help homeowners decide if the project they are contemplating is affordable and worth pursuing with a reliable contractor.

Roofing costs, for example, are fairly standard. Shingles are sold and installed by the "square," which is the amount of shingles required to cover 100 square feet of roof. The smallest increment is one-third of a square. A typical home may measure out to over twenty squares. Roofers charge by the square. The pitch of the roof also factors into the cost – the steeper the roof, the steeper the price. Gutter costs so much per lineal foot. The problem with remodeling is additional work aside from new shingles is usually required. Chimney caps and vents may be rusted beyond repair, existing shingles may need to be removed, and sheathing and trim may have rotted if the roof is especially bad. New attic vents are sometimes added. If the work being considered is comparable to a new roof, with minor additional work, a few estimates from reliable contractors will establish a realistic price range for the owner.

Or, ask about drywall costs. Drywall is figured into the job costs on a per sheet basis. Homeowners may see it at the lumberyard for $5 per sheet. A contractor may charge $50 per sheet. He figures in the cost of the board, delivery, hanging, cost of screws and fasteners, corner bead, scaffolding, equipment, joint compound, tape, finishing, texture, scaffolding, equipment, crews, insurance, scrapping out, and profit and overhead to arrive at that $50 per sheet figure. In simple figures, if an addition requires 50 sheets, the drywall bill will be around $2,500.

Smart consumers will shop prices and compare before jumping into a purchase. The only difference between a big screen TV and a bay window is this: The stakes are much higher with a window. If a TV breaks, it goes back to the shop. If the window installation goes awry, part of a family's prime investment could go with it.

If the remodel project is a major one, requiring a "team" consisting of an owner, architect, and contractor, it is foolish to not establish a budget and make that figure well-known to all of the involved parties. The owners who establish their spending limit from the outset will be sending a clear message to the architect and builder and has just increased their odds of being happy owners when the project is done.

There is a big difference between saving money and doing things cheaply. Good contractors, on the whole, refuse to do things cheaply. The implication, of course, is that if you are doing things cheaply you have a bad contractor.

This scenario happens all the time: A project is planned out, a price range is established, and the homeowners receive a final and complete estimate for the entire job. Last-minute additions, like the wine rack in the basement and stained glass over the stairs, are accounted for. Sticker shock turns their faces white. Incoherent mumbling follows. Not long after they can string together complete sentences, they say, "This is more than we wanted to spend. How can we get this cost down?"

In their panic stricken eyes you can see what they really want you to say is this: "You are two of the nicest people I have ever met. I really want you to have a nice addition, so here's what I'll do. You see that 30% figure, for profit and overhead, that you keep pointing out to each other and whispering about? All that money is supposed to go into my pocket, where it doesn't do you a bit of good. I know it's a chunk of change, so let's cut that out. I'll take all the risk and work for nothing! I'm serious. I was planning on going out of business after this job anyway."

But do they want to heart his from their contractor? "You are two of the nicest people I've ever met. I've worked real hard to get this job, and I've carefully calculated every unit of trim and every dumpster load, and then I've added an extra 30% to the cost of everything on top of my 30% profit and overhead. I was hoping it wouldn't be an issue, but can see from the look on your faces I'll have to knock this down a little bit. Frankly, your house is a disaster to begin with and I know you're having trouble getting bids from other contractors. For me, this would be a nice job to have. Lucky for you I've padded everything way too much. Besides, I'm making way too much money off my other clients, the poor suckers. I can take 15% off right now, take it or leave it."

And how would this sit in your stomach? "You are two of the nicest people I've ever met, and I really want to do this job. I think if we cut some corners here and there we can get the price down. This permit cost bugs me. That's a lot of money to spend, plus it's always a hassle dealing with the city. Costs time and money. With no permits, I know some guys who could do it on the side and do it cheap. You'd have to sign some waivers, which is no big deal..."

Here's what homeowners can expect to hear from a good contractor: "I've double and triple-checked all my figures. The only padding might be in the contingency fund, and we don't want to knock that down any. The first place we start is with the wine rack and the stained glass. You can do those next year when you're more flush. And if you deal directly with my subs they'll do a good job and you'll save some money, too. The windows spec'd by the architect are kind of expensive. I'd like you to consider this other line. They are very nice and they'll look good with the house. I think we could save a couple of thousand dollars there. And if the bathroom lay-out was different, we wouldn't have to move all of the existing plumbing. That's about a $1500 savings. And if we dropped the new roof to butt up against the old house instead of planing it out to match the existing, we wouldn't have to tear off the old shingles and sheathing and re-roof the entire house. When the roofer was here I had him price that as an alternate, and you're looking at a $5,000 savings."

Bad contractors who do things cheaply don't protect furnishings, don't clean up after themselves, place new finishes over inadequate or unprepared substrates, skimp on materials, neglect all the little details that distinguish a good job from a crappy job, don't follow through on problems, may leave homeowners liable to claims from injured workers, risk red-tagging their homes, and are a good fit with Homeowners from Hell looking for a cheap job.

The Lifetime Achievement Award for Homeowners from Hell should be named after Shah Jahan, an Indian ruler of the seventeenth century. He was best known for constructing a tomb in honor of his favorite wife, an edifice we all know as the Taj Mahal. Begun in 1630, the project took 20,000 men 18 years to complete. To ensure that a rival building would never be constructed, the hands of all of the master builders were chopped off when the project was completed. The architect was beheaded. I hope the punchlist was already completed.

Once I priced finishing one room in one basement. It was a 12'x12' bedroom. The walls were already drywalled and all I had to figure was providing and installing a couple of doors, casing and hardware for the doors, and base. The price included stain and finish. I gave the owner a simpleton estimate and he frowned. This is about how the conversation went:

Owner: "This is more than I planned on spending."

Me: "I priced the exact same trim as the rest of the house. It's 50 cents a foot. The doors are $30 each. Matching knobs are $12. I can do the trim in one day – pickup materials, hang doors, run trim and cleanup. The next day, I'll stain and finish everything. That's two days labor, total."

Owner: "How much would I save if I picked up the materials myself?"

He's thinking I'm screwing him on the cost of materials.

Me: "All of the labor cost. I wouldn't commit to doing the job unless I supplied the materials. That way, I know I won't run short or the materials won't be defective. Plus, it's only saving an hour out of my day." *Like*

I'm going to watch "The View" with the extra hour.

Owner: "How much would I save if we went with hollow core doors and finger joint trim?"

Only idiots stain finger joint trim. This confirmed I was dealing with one.

Me: "I don't know for sure. Maybe $40."

Owner: "If I went with finger joint trim and hollow doors, and then stained everything myself and hired you to apply the sealer, how much would I save?"

As far as I was concerned, we were just doing word problems out loud at this point. He lost me. I wasn't going to refigure a dinky job ten times.

Me: "Maybe $106.45."

His eyes brightened. Now he was getting somewhere.

Owner: "So if I do the staining and we use the less expensive trim and I clean up after you, how much could I save then?"

Me: "You can save the cost of the whole job, because I'm not doing it."

The "job down the road" is an elusive mirage everyone in the construction business hears at one time or another. "Give me a break on the cost," goes the refrain, and "I'll make you sure you get that great job down the road." Let me rip you you off, and the implication is that there will be an unending supply of work that will more than make up for this temporary inconvenience to your checkbook. The truth is, the only way contractors turn that mirage into reality is through good service, integrity, and satisfied clients. Longtime clients who are a good source of referrals get a break on my costs, not first-timers.

Some homeowners try to avoid the mark-up that plumbers, electricians, and other tradesmen and contractors charge on faucets, spas, lights, and other fixtures. Homeowners see a comparable item in a "Big Box" store at a considerable savings, and ask why they don't supply the fixtures themselves and save money? On some projects, the savings on a lot of items can really add up.

This is a double-edged sword.

Plumbers, for example, usually have established relations with various suppliers who warranty their products and have a network of sales representatives who deal with problems. Plumbers get fixtures and parts at wholesale prices and resell them to the consumer at a standard mark-up. If a plumber supplies a kitchen faucet that cost him $90, he may charge the homeowner $125. Suppose the homeowner knows he could pick up the exact same item for $100.

If the plumber supplies the faucet, and it proves to be defective, he should repair or replace it at no charge. If the owner supplies the faucet, and it proves to be defective, he can expect to pay for a service call, possibly equaling or exceeding the cost of the faucet.

A defective faucet can be a small problem. A fiberglass bathtub that begins to crack a few months after installation can be a major headache. Settling and shrinkage may occur in the framing lumber supporting the tub if the floor is inadequate. Most tubs should be set in a pan of mud or plaster to provide uniform support. If everything is not done just right, hair-line cracks can show up in the finish. Who fixes what? This is when the Blame Game begins.

The supplier says the tub was not properly installed. The plumber says it was, but the contractor should have made the carpenter beef up the joists. The contractor says the joists are adequate, and the tub is defective. The manufacturer hires someone to repair the cracks, and the repairs look worse than the cracks. Eventually, after numerous trips through the bathroom by half a dozen tradesmen and factory representatives, the manufacturer agrees to supply a new tub. Not because the tub is defective, but because the manufacturer has the deepest pockets. Now there's a brand new tub in the garage. If the plumber didn't supply it, he's going to charge to put it in. Someone has to call the tile setter to rip out and replace the lower courses of tile. And what about the floor? Is the contractor going to beef it up for free? And if he decides to strengthen the floor after all, does this mean the floor was inadequate in the first place? These are good questions to ask your builder before the bathroom begins, not four months after the project is over.

Most tradesmen will install owner-provided items with the proviso that if the part chips, breaks, or short-circuits they will not (understandably) warrant a product they haven't supplied.

Owners and architects shouldn't lose sight of the fact that subcontractors are a good source of information about the products they install. An architect or designer may specify a product they have seen at a home show or in a magazine or catalog. But the plumber or electrician will know if this is a solid choice. Often times, they can recommend an alternative fixture that saves money and is less subject to callbacks.

Owners have every right to select their own products. Owners who also want to provide materials need to make arrangements while the contract is being written. Some subs oppose homeowners who choose to do business this way, especially if the owner wants to supply every fixture on the job. Professionals know the intricacies of ordering fixtures and sometimes resent the intrusion into their business and their checkbook. Homeowners frequently purchase items that don't fit or are incomplete. This causes frustrating and time-consuming delays, usually at a critical juncture in the job.

Tile from a discount store, for example, often has blemishes, size, and color variations detectable only to the installer who is responsible for the finished product. A lot of discounted tile are considered "seconds." Installing "seconds" makes his job harder

Most subcontractors want to install a quality product and move on to the next job. All tradesmen do their best to avoid callbacks. Homeowners sometimes only look at the price, which in this instance is not the bottom line.

Check with your contractor and subs. Buy your own if you're cautious and feeling lucky.

Happy homeowners have realistic expectations about how a project will turn out. Homeowners who wind up at the opposite end of the spectrum don't. Ray N___ was renovating a large space for his small business. 80 years before, the space was a dairy and the floors were actually glazed tiles. The tiles, however, looked like a typical 4"x 8" garden paver with a slight glaze. This particular space was nearly 2,000 square feet, and part of the renovation required me to patch a few square feet here and there where pipes had been abandoned.

The building was located in a century old urban district that was undergoing an economic revival. Boutiques and sports bars were displacing pawn shops and winos. Old brick structures were rebuilt, windows were replaced and filled in, and crumbling masonry was patched back together. A blind man could see where a window was filled in on one of these buildings. Replacement bricks, while similar, were never an exact match. Neither was the mortar or the mason's technique. I told Ray I'd match the floor tiles as best I could and that would have to do.

I went to every salvage yard in town, couldn't find an exact match, and selected some garden pavers that were pretty close. I colored the mud to match the existing dark gray joints and added a few coats of sealer to create a bit of a shine on the tiles to mimic the worn glazing on the old tiles. The newer pavers weren't quite as dark as the originals, but I was happy with how it turned out.

Ray went ballistic when he saw what I had done. If he looked at the patches and casually remarked that he didn't like them, I might have sympathized with him (although I totally disagreed.) Instead, he was as animated as a cartoon character out of the Warner Brothers Studio. Ray's meltdown tagged him as a client who the forces of reason would be lost upon. Clearly, this was a little man with big troubles.

He insisted he wouldn't pay until the blunder was corrected. I told him to look around the city because it was impossible to get an exact match on masonry that old. I also told him a few other things.

We soon found an architect who "mediated" the matter. He worked around the corner, and his fee was lunch, paid by the loser. Ray aired his grievances and I know the architect did his very best to maintain some degree of professionalism and keep a straight face as Ray presented his case. The arbitrator ruled in my favor and Ray went out of business the following year. The current tenants would be dumbfounded to learn the amount of conversation that went into those few square feet of flooring.

Had Ray taken the time to stroll around the block and examine his surroundings more closely, he may have gained some realistic expectations about building and some insight about business...

Honorable Mention

"This is twice as high as the estimate," Ms. C___ said to Earl. "Jill" was looking over the bill as Earl B___ was picking up his tools. They were standing in the garage, their bodies awash in the late afternoon sun that cast a golden hue on the lawn mower and weed eater. Hang dog Earl was dead tired. The new garage door had been a difficult project from the get-go.

The estimator had failed to notice the dry-rot that made the existing jambs totally worthless. Earl couldn't blame him. It was under a dozen layers of paint. Earl didn't even notice it until he ran a three inch screw into the wood and the whole board crumbled.

Earl was in a bind. The old door was just trash – it was coming down in pieces. He was so booked up he couldn't do it tomorrow or even come back the next day just to finish. And forget about leaving the garage door open all night – the garage was full of golf clubs and bikes.

"Jill" was gone for most of the day. She didn't leave a number, and he had no way to tell her he had to drop what he was doing, run to the lumberyard and pick up 2x12's, tear out the old jambs, and install new ones. He left before lunch and didn't get the new jambs in until after 2:00.

The fine print on the contract stated the homeowner was responsible for extras and unseen conditions, and this extra was common in older homes.

Earl reckoned it must have been 100 degrees outside with humidity to match. His dark blue polyester coveralls just cooked him to death on days like this. The rollers on the old door were full of grease and metal filings, and by the end of the day his hands were black.

He just knew he was a mess.

"Jill" slowly paced through the garage while she studied the bill. She was a naturally bleached blonde, artificially tanned, and had returned from her errands wearing a sleeveless blouse, khaki shorts, and flip-flops. Her hair was tied back in a ponytail. Compared to Earl, she looked crisp and clean. Earl wasn't much of a guesser, but he figured she was in her mid-thirties.

"Jill" noticed Earl had pulled out every tool in his truck to get her door in, and she complimented him on how smoothly it operated. She knew she could have gotten a cheaper job from another company, but her father had left her the house in perfect condition and she knew her Dad would have hired the best. The firm Earl worked for had a spotless reputation for 30 years, and that was worth a lot to Jill. She had hoped to spend about $500 for a new door, but the estimate came in at $630. Now, with these extras, the bill was close to $1,000.

"I've itemized the extras," Earl said as he stopped a moment to smear a sweaty black streak across his brow. He pointed out the figures on the signed work order Jill cradled against her bosom.

"The lumber for the new jambs was $50, lags and fasteners an extra $10, and then I had another three hours in the job over and above the estimate. The company rate is $70 an hour. This includes picking up material, removing the old jambs, and installing the new ones. I also shimmed 'em good so you've got a nice tight fit."

She seemed resigned to the bill. "I understand," "Jill" said. "These things happen."

"Just look at this," Earl said as he picked up the old jamb leg and held it out. "Look at it," he repeated as he crumbled the rotted lumber between his thumb and forefinger, then tossed it back into the truck with a finality that announced he was done for the day.

"Jill" shook her head, then took another step toward Earl. It might have been the first moment all day he stopped moving, and he let out an exhausted sigh. In the bright light, up close, Earl noticed a greenish tinge to her blue eyes.

"God, you must be hot," "Jill" said. "Let me fix you some lemonade."

That was an offer he couldn't refuse. He followed her through the garage and up into the kitchen. She motioned for him to sit down while she rummaged through the freezer. "This will take a few minutes," she said. "Why don't you go get cleaned up a bit if you want to. The bathroom's just down the hall. You must be exhausted and you've worked so hard. There's plenty of towels in there if you want to take a shower, " she said brightly.

Earl looked up, somewhat puzzled, while "Jill" shut the freezer door.

"If you don't cool off some, it'll be a long ride home..."

Earl looked down at the wood grained laminate table top. He absent-mindedly ran a blackened fingertip along the imitation grain. The little angel on his left shoulder told him to get up and get in his truck and drive straight home. The little devil on his right shoulder told him he was a dirty mess and better jump in the shower before he stunk up the whole kitchen. And besides, what harm is there in accepting some hospitality?

He stood, exhausted and unsteady, and walked down the hall to the bathroom.

As soon as he got under the cooling needles he knew he had made the right choice. Shampoo ran down his body in grayish gobs at first, swirling in the drain, then turning to clear foam.

He got a start when the door opened. It shut a moment later and he peeked around the heavy shower curtain, relieved to see the bathroom was empty.

Earl didn't notice his clothes were gone until he was toweling off. "Jill?" he hollered through the door. "Where are my clothes? Jill?"

Her voice was right outside the door. "I threw them in the wash. I hope you don't mind. It's the quick cycle. They should be dried in about 45 minutes. I put all the screws and change in a saucer. I left you that lemonade."

Earl picked the glass off the shelf and drank until the ice bounced off his lip. He wrapped the towel around his middle and stepped into the hall. "Jill" greeted him like a fresh breeze. She took the empty glass from his hand.

"My, don't you clean up nice," she said as she looked him up and down. She placed her hand on his bare chest. "You still seem pretty warm, Earl. Here, let me get you a refill."

From the kitchen she yelled, "I think there's an old robe in the bedroom that's close to your size, Earl. Go look on the closet door, on the inside. This lemonade's coming right up."

Earl had the robe in one hand and the towel in the other when Jill returned. She set both lemonades on the bed stand, kicked off her flip-flops, and closed the door...

"Jill" called before dawn the next morning. The sweet, musical voice was gone. In its stead was a thin, empty monotone. For a moment, Earl doubted it was the same person. But then she recounted yesterday evening's cheap sex like she was reading aloud from the obituaries. A deep sense of dread grabbed his heart with both hands and wouldn't let go.

"You tell them, Earl. You tell them you screwed up. You tell them whatever you have to say to get that bill down to $500 or you'll be facing rape charges. There's still plenty of evidence around here, you know what I mean. Do you want me to tell the boss about that tattoo on your ass? I don't think so."

Looking back, Earl always wondered what she saw in him.

Earl threw away the receipts and called in sick that day. He told his supervisor he became ill yesterday afternoon while he was installing Ms.C___'s door and promised he would get her a discount down to $500 if she arranged to haul everything off and clean up. Earl was a long-time employee, and his supervisor told him to take it easy and look after himself.

Psychotic Remodeling

16

I'M DUE AND MY FLOOR IS AT AN ACUTE ANGLE

Sometimes it's the things that go bump in the night that give us the worst start of all.

A few of us went out on a service call early one morning to an apartment complex in a tiny municipality surrounded by a major metropolitan area. Something about a floor. We knocked on the door of the first floor apartment and a weary young couple let us in. He was young and dark-haired with a medium build, and if he wasn't unshaved with his hair falling over his red eyes, and if he wasn't wearing old sweats, he might have been described as "clean-cut." His bedraggled wife's hair hung in limp brown strands at this early hour, her tired eyes concealed by the large glasses you knew she only wore around the house. She was tall and thin, wearing her nightgown, trying to pull an old robe around her stomach. Most of her difficulty stemmed from the fact that she was nine months pregnant, due any day, and her fashion options were limited.

The apartment was nice enough, but the dresser and nightstands sure seemed out of place in the living room.

"Are we glad you guys showed up," Tom W___ said as we introduced ourselves. "Take a look back here."

He ushered us through the hallway and into the bedroom. I had never seen anything like it.

One entire end of the floor had dropped into the crawl space. The foot of the bed was parked at the bottom of the floor against the foundation wall. The crawl space was about three feet deep and the room was about fifteen square feet. A three foot drop in fifteen feet roughly translates to about just over ten degrees. Definitely an acute angle.

We all stared at the bed. Then, in unison, we turned to Tom. "It didn't slide down there instantly," he said. "I woke up in the middle of the night from this...jolt ." He gestured with his hands held his in front of him as if he were describing a bosomy woman running down a flight of stairs. "That must have been when the floor dropped, in that corner over there. At first, I thought we were having an earthquake. I could hear the wood tearing, so I grabbed Janie and we got out of the bed on this side.When we got to the door, the whole thing just went WHOOMPH!, and then the bed eased on down."

He looked at Janie, one glance highlighting her delicate condition. "We're OK, thank God we got out of there in time. The neighbor helped move some of this stuff out, but he had to go to work. I couldn't handle the bed myself. I called the management company and left a message right away. I guess you guys have a contract with them."

It didn't take much for three carpenters fueled by a gallon of coffee to take the bed apart and stack it in a corner of the living room. We gingerly stepped on the floor, not quite sure what had happened and not yet sure how deep the hole was. A closer inspection along the outside wall told us what had happened:

Moisture had accumulated in the crawl space because there were no vents in the foundation wall. Over just a few years (the complex was ten years old) dry rot had set in. The 2"x 10" framing lumber achieved a styrofoam-like consistency before it gave way in the middle of the night. We were literally tearing the wood apart with our bare hands, chucking it out the bedroom window. In the corner that initially tore loose, about three feet of each joist had completely rotted; only a foot had rotted at the other end of the wall.

This particular city, in order to encourage high density residential development, used a building code book about the size of an Archie Comic. No crawl space ventilation had been provided for. Then moisture built up and rotted the floor at an early age.

We were able to replace the floor (sans carpet) by the end of the day and move the bedroom set back where it belonged. Then we spent another month installing crawl space vents in 64 ground-level units.

The three of us kept checking in with the expectant parents to make sure the carpet arrived, but they moved out shortly after their floor was rebuilt. We never learned the baby's name, or even saw it, but we're sure it was a cute one.

17

PUBLIC ENEMY #1

There is no escaping this thing that surrounds us.

An entire legal industry is devoted to its rights. It batters our homes and sweeps them aside in moments, yet usually breaks and enters through pinhole-sized passageways. It can destroy our homes with a terminal, unthinking, and unblinking tenacity. It is a changeling, *a shape shifter*, mutating with ease from a hard thing buried in the ground one moment to a nebulous cloud the next.

While we do all we can to protect ourselves from it, we spend billions of dollars annually to bring it into our homes. We pipe, drain, filter and divert it. We drill thousands of feet into the earth to find it, and remodel the natural world to store it. As we continue to wrestle with it, we ultimately find we are battling ourselves.

If the Earth is a living organism, as some people suggest, then water is the sweat and tears of the world.

Water inflicts more damage to more homes than any other single source.

(Note: Natural disasters like hurricanes, tidal waves, and horrible flooding are destructive forces that have ruined and snuffed out millions of lives. *Psychotic Remodeling* doesn't care to compete with Hollywood in dramatizing or trivializing a serious and deadly topic. Yet the terrible statistics they are responsible for are taken into account in the course of this chapter.)

Snow freezes and thaws, inexorably creating tiny cracks and fissures in all but the slickest surfaces. In temperate climates, these tiny cracks

131

widen with each freeze-thaw cycle, and soon water has found a handhold to your home. This opening may be tucked into the corner of the patio, where the slab meets the brick wall, or on the roof at the flat shady spot alongside the chimney. Freeze-thaw can cause spalling and flaking in improperly laid concrete. Roof eaves and gutters are especially suscepti-ble to this unavoidable process. Before long, water gets behind the gutter, beneath the fascia, and lays on the top of the soffit to puddle a while before running down the wall and damaging original artwork.

Water can wash out the soil beneath concrete, (homes don't float too well), contribute to mold in the back of the closet, run through roof pen-etrations and skylights, get behind tile to rot walls and floors, cause stains in new wallpaper, rot framing lumber, buckle wood floors and trim, attack exterior paint in certain climates, attract bugs, and wear out and corrode plumbing fixtures and pipes on a regular basis.

Ancient alchemists believed the Earth was composed of four ele-ments – earth, wind, fire, and water. Maintaining a balance between the benefits of these "elements" and guarding against their destructive poten-tial is a constant process. Homeowners must be vigilant to keep their res-idences watertight and safe. But even a perfectly maintained home is sus-ceptible to the ravages of water.

Most of us love to listen to the rain or the sound of water. It evokes a primeval connection with the natural world. Men and women can find it romantic; untold numbers of artists and composers are inspired by the stirring natural cacophonies of lightning and thunder sweeping across the heavens. Yet homeowners cringe if they know their home is wounded and unable to face the elements alone.

Over time, the sound of the elements tinkling or dripping caused dread to surface in the heart of Allan P___. The owner of a brand new home, he confessed to me that he broke into tears and sobbed during the middle of his first night in the cursed house.

In terms of sheer economics, the place was a steal. Overall, it was a nightmare. The property was finished shortly before the recession, and sat on a corner lot in a prominent high-end development for many months. Money was tight, interest rates were rising, jobs were scarce, and the housing market had dried up. The developer had to dump it.

It was a handsome white stucco with a concrete tile roof. A nice move up home if your goal is a $500,000 house. The problem was, everything leaked. The roof, the windows, the foundation, and the exterior walls offered no resistance to the forces of nature.

On that first night, a heavy storm rolled in from the north. The sky blackened late in the afternoon and bore down upon the unsuspecting new owner before he had unpacked much more than a bed.

Winds battered the rain sideways into his home. A fierce electrical storm that lit up the night gave way to a series of sodden, mournful showers. Water pooled on all the window sills and then ran downhill into the basement, streaking the bare concrete walls until their entire breadth glistened from the leaks above.

The drains deep in the wells of the basement windows were never connected properly, their fittings smashed from gravel, the perimeter drain undulating up and down like a series of low, rolling hills. The sump pit, designed to collect this water, was always dry.

After midnight, water began to rise above the window sills. By dawn, the windows held back two feet of water as best they could, the liquid fear spritzing through the weatherstripping.

Smelling the wet concrete, hearing the windows hiss, he felt his home sink into the muck.

Dryer and vent penetrations were not flashed and caulked, the number of downspouts was inadequate for the amount of roof, and the stucco detail around the windows was not installed strictly to the manufacturer's specifications. Some of the weatherstripping on the windows was removed to allow room for the metal cladding. When the alarm guy drilled holes for his sensors in the bottom of the now leaking window sills, he created a perfect trap door in each window for water to run down the walls and into the basement.

And the roofers!

Originally, the house was going to have a cedar shake roof. At the last minute, cedar was changed to a concrete tile. The crew worked on a weekend and their installation was never inspected "mid-roof." They eliminated flashing and felt where it suited them. Bear in mind that flashing and felt is what keeps the house watertight. Concrete shingles only protect the flashing and felt and provide a nicer architectural detail to a half-million dollar home than tar-paper could ever accomplish.

The battens that kept the tiles off the tar paper were skewed and diverted water to gaping holes alongside the chimney and second story walls. Once water finds a pathway into a home, a trickle soon develops into a stream, and if the problem isn't corrected soon enough, you're looking at the Grand Canyon several times over as water carves its way behind the walls.

Nervous! That's what Allan was. Whenever snow melt dribbled down the roof on a sunny afternoon or a spring shower greened up the flower beds, he searched the windows and took photos of the basement walls with a dull blue eye. His scrapbook, every print carefully dated, chronicled the fall of his house into the maelstrom.

We often stood in deadened silence, Allan wondering aloud if I heard the tell tale trickle behind the walls.

Allan was certain that water droplets conspired at night on how to best inflict their misery on him.

He lived about three aeronautical miles to the south of my home, and when thunderheads built up after work and a storm pounded the region to the south, I knew my pager would soon vibrate as Allan endeavored to provide a verbal record of the indignities inflicted upon him as he sat awash in a sea of leaks.

I felt sorry for him, now unable to enjoy the cooling, transcendental soothing of a summer shower from the comfort of his bed, by many accounts one of life's little pleasures.

We all felt sorry for him. The builder, the window guy, the building inspector, and the neighbors. My turn to tackle his leaks eventually surfaced in the natural order of things, and by the time my shift was over his home was impervious to all but the worst storms. On one occasion the building inspector, due to Allan's conniving, ambushed the roofer in his front yard. He threatened to shut all of his jobs down unless the roof was corrected by the end of the month.

Every window was carefully examined by a rep from the window manufacturer, and weather stripping was reinstalled. The alarm sensors were moved to the top of the windows, their holes plugged and caulked. Another 589 tubes of caulk sealed around any and all vent penetrations, windows, and exterior lights, especially the ones that had one-half inch romex cable protruding from fist-sized holes behind the fixtures. More downspouts were added. The holes from eight inch gutter spikes that perforated the fascia board were sealed with silicone caulk. Perimeter drains were dug up by crews that tunneled ten feet below the lawn's surface, and reconnected. Concrete slabs were topped with flagstone, their new veneers pitched to ensure positive drainage. Self-leveling polyurethane caulk sealed the slabs tight to the house. Window wells were dug out and flashed where heavy timbers had punctured the foam behind the stucco. A second story deck was partially torn up, the planking under the sliding door properly flashed. Stucco repairs were made.

There were probably over 200 distinct and separate leaks that contributed to Allan's nightmare, and it took a couple of years to sort through them all. The tide was turned a drip at a time. Now his home is impervious to all but the most sustained deluges, but it may be a while until he sleeps through a drizzle.

I drove past his house last week, and noticed it was for sale. The disclosure statement should make fine reading.

Dr. R___ was a world traveler from a foreign land. He eventually settled with his family in an exclusive suburban enclave in the United States, where he was the neighbor to world famous celebrities. His own star shone brightly through his scientific work. The Dr.'s expertise was the field of mold, an unattractive subject to most people, yet he was a man of vision and opportunity who translated this seemingly distasteful field into an enterprise of culinary delight.

When a pure culture of lactic acid bacteria (mold) is added to fresh milk, it separates into solids (curd), and liquid (whey). The curd is separated, heated, ripened with more molds, and (I'm condensing the process quite a bit) voila – cheese! The flavor of some cheese, like roquefort and cheddar, is enhanced when additional molds are added during the production process, before they are pressed into forms and cured. Dr. R___ was the CEO of a far-flung cheese empire with factories in the Midwest, Great Britain, and Europe. He oversaw every step of the production process, from the source of the milk to the condition of the equipment, because his client required a uniform product.

Dr. R___'s cheese supplied the largest pizza chains in the United States and their worldwide network of franchises. He was often required to tinker with his formulas to achieve the upper hand in the cut-throat world of the pizza business. (Leaving more water in the cheese, for example, causes the cheese topping to brown quicker. M-mmmm.)

This brilliant man – who could wax enthusiastically about cheese to anyone who happened by, clearly wasn't doing too bad for himself. So it was a surprise when he spoke to me in semi-confidential tones one day, "My wife, you know, she comes from a very well-off family. They have many real-estate holdings where they live."

With a builder's professional camaraderie, she showed us the plans of their home on the other side of the world that was nearly complete. Most Americans would call it a palace.

It's too bad the U.S. house we were standing in was the biggest disaster I had ever seen.

At one time it was beautiful. The residence was nearly six thousand square feet. In this shopping mall of a house, tucked in the back corner, was the original dwelling, a farmhouse of a thousand square feet. It was originally built in the 1920's, in rolling countryside at a high enough elevation to view over one hundred miles of the Rocky Mountains from north to south. Over the decades the surrounding land became urbanized, yet this particular spot never lost its country charm until the late 1970's when developers began to colonize the area with four and five thousand square foot homes.

From the remaining furnishings and decor, it was clear that the home most closely resembled a museum before the disaster hit. The foyer was marble tile with a twenty foot ceiling and a massive glitzy chandelier in the center. At the far end was a twelve foot wide staircase that led to the second floor. The solid brass railings and glass panels beneath wrapped above the foyer on three sides, creating a mezzanine that led to the bedrooms upstairs. Ms. R___ showed us a picture of the foyer before the disaster, which happened to be on the cover of a national magazine.

Most of the furnishings and salvageable artwork had been removed by the clean-up crews, but in one corner sat an enormous and forlorn Buddha's bust. It was about five feet tall, and hand carved from a massive block of teak. The detail and intricacies of the carvings – every ringlet of hair on his head was shaved to perfect detail – was belied by the massive crack that cleaved his skull to the bridge of the nose.

The moisture content of the room, combined with the heat, and then the eventual drying out, turned this five-figure treasure into little more than scrap lumber.

Now, all that was left in the musty remains of their home of objects d'art was wet sponge carpeting and miscellaneous furnishings.

The insurance settlement for the furnishings was rumored to run into the millions. And it could have been much higher. All for a fifty-nine cent nut.

Upstairs, off the master bedroom, was a gazebo shaped sitting area. The peaked ceiling and window-lined walls were covered with a sheer white fabric, lending a translucent, almost ephemeral transcendence to the interior of the turret. In the corner of this room was a small wet bar, its faucet piped with water by two 3/8" copper supply tubes attached to the shut-off valves. It was a standard installation. Small nuts, when combined with a compression sleeve that slips on the outside of the copper supply lines, make a watertight connection when they are screwed to the threaded end of the valve. No one knew for sure what caused the nut to crack. It's possible it was overtightened at some point and the plumber didn't notice a leak, or tightened enough to cause a hairline fracture that was unnoticeable at the time. Although the exact cause was unclear, the results were very apparent.

Water began to trickle out from around the nut at first, and a small but persistent stream gradually worked its way into a steady flow. Had anyone been home to notice the leak in time, all they needed to do was simply turn off the valve and call the plumber. Actually, almost any Do-It-Yourselfer could have fixed the leak.

But no one was home. The R___'s were on the other side of the world when their nut cracked. Evidently the person who normally checked on the house didn't notice it at first, (the house was huge, after all) and missed a couple of other checks due to a family emergency. Through a tragedy of errors, checking on the house was postponed for a few days; the R___'s were due home soon anyway, but were then delayed.

A week passed.

When Dr. R___ finally made it home one afternoon in the middle of winter, the first hint of disaster came when he opened the garage doors and a tidal bore of water rushed at his Mercedes. The three car garage was directly under the gazebo-style room off the master bedroom, and held about two feet of water. The Jaguar convertible inside was drowned; during the estimating process, Dr. R___hinted that he would let the coupe go for a song.

From the wet bar, water ran into the adjacent master bedroom and the dining room below. We eventually pulled that ceiling down. Too bad it was covered with mirrors. The wall-to-wall carpeting wicked up enough water to leave a soggy mess in the master bathroom just past the bedroom.

The kitchen was below the bathroom and water collected over the kitchen in the joist bays. Water ran out of ceiling fixtures, drywall screwholes, and the huge melon-sized blisters that formed in the skin of paint on the kitchen ceiling. Dirty water dripped through every kitchen cabinet. Pots and pans were rusting. The R___'s were so distraught and dismayed that they couldn't even conceive of preparing or eating another meal in this room. Ms. R___ shuddered at the thought

The back stairwell off the kitchen led downstairs. During the course of the leak, this served as the Grand Waterfall. Water cascaded down the slate tiled steps, hit the landing, and then turned into the exquisitely finished basement that now sat in ruins.

At the bottom of the stairs, to the right, was a sleek bar and kitchen. To the left was a spare bedroom and bath. Continuing past the kitchen was the main room, its walls and columns faux-painted marble to resemble an ancient city. Unfortunately, that city was now in the submerged continent of Atlantis.

An elaborate wine cellar on the left was now empty, its vessels safely stored. Past the wine cellar on the far wall was a tiled fireplace and built-in, sunken, (formerly submerged) sitting area. Mirrors lined the opposite end of the room. Judging by the bath-tub ring around the walls, about three feet of standing water sloshed through before making its way to the floor drain under the original farmhouse another fifty feet to the east.

The utility department, comparing normal usage against the recorded flow, estimated 87,000 gallons rained through the house over a five day period.

Surprisingly, most damage was caused not by the water but by the humidity. The primary furnace in the basement, its ductwork branching out all over the main floor, proved to be little more than a water collection system. It soon shorted out as water drained through its ductwork and flooded the basement.

Because it was the dead of winter, the other furnaces (on the main level in the back of the house and an upstairs furnace) continued to cycle on and off. They ran more than usual to compensate for their drowned comrade, heating all the moisture in the air and turning their home into a steam bath. The hot water heater ran constantly. Dr. R___ told us the humidity levels were over 100%! These conditions are perfect for peeling wallpaper off the walls, de-laminating cabinets, and causing every electrical device to oxidize. Stereos, TV's, switches, plugs, fans, speakers, appliances, fixtures they were all shot.

The finish on the cabinets was literally steamed off. In order to replace the cabinets, the granite tops that had been glued on would have to come off in one piece. Not likely. Then, the slate floor had to be torn up to replace the ruined substrate. The entire kitchen would have to be re-done. Now multiply this amount of work by the size of the rest of the house to get some sense of the complexity of the job. Untangling and separating what was directly water-damaged from what was damaged by association was a Herculean task.

Marble and ceramic tile was the predominate finish material, and the plywood substrate had swollen due to the high humidity levels, causing tiles to pop off. Mirrored ceilings and walls became suspect, since their substrate was now unreliable. The plywood under the carpeting was swollen and blistered, and had to be replaced. All of the door joints were cracked, since the house cooked in a steam shower for nearly a week.

Despite this disaster, the current condition of his home was not his main worry.

Shortly after he left on his trip, his insurance policy was canceled.

The cancellation notice arrived in the mail probably about the same time the house sprung a leak. Dr. R___ had made too many nuisance claims with the company – almost as though he expected the insurance company to perform maintenance on his home. His policy was canceled.

The local agent was co-operative and understanding. He paid to clean up the mess, store what was salvageable, and found temporary lodging for the family (they had a son in college) in a modest 3,000 square foot home less than five minutes away. We walked the national representative through the house after we did a complete estimate of what we thought was needed to restore the home, and he disallowed 75% of the actual construction work, which added up to a few hundred thousand dollars.

Time was of the essence, and a time-consuming lawsuit was not on the immediate agenda. They reached a settlement and did a cheapo fixer-upper on the place. The insurance company replaced personal possessions and popped for new drywall, some trim, new carpet and wallpaper. Basically, they paid to redecorate instead of reconstruct.

I don't know how it eventually turned out, because we never got the contract. Our expertise was in high-end remodel, and a good job is not a cheap job. The insurance company was more inclined toward cheap than good, and we were out of the picture after bidding $500,000 in repairs – a very time-consuming process. Dr. R___ never returned our calls, and we know he was infinitely embarrassed over the entire episode, having unwittingly led us on.

I have a feeling he put the place on the market as soon as it was patched back together.

Nowadays, sensors are available that can be installed near potential disasters. These sensors are wired to an electronic valve at the house's water main, and can shut the system down before things get out of hand. Washing machine hookups fail more often than most people suspect – electronic valves that plug into a standard outlet are now available that supply water only when the machine is running.

High humidity levels contribute to the conditions that are ripe for mold. Dr. R___ was one of the foremost authorities on the subject of mold in the entire world.

In the dining room ceiling we tore down, the mirrored one, little green blotches had appeared in just a few weeks. The insurance company told us a fungicide would take care of it, but Dr. R___ didn't believe it. And most of the framing lumber was saturated with moisture at one time or another with no way to completely dry out. The insurance company assured us everything would dry safely without adequate ventilation.

Off hand, I can think of one young couple besides the R___'s who would dispute that claim.

Mike J___ is now a retired builder. Not an old man by any means, he was in search of new challenges and much less brain damage after his last few building projects. Although we both enjoy construction on one level, we share a jaundiced eye toward the peculiarities of the building profession.

Mike was a good source for this project. He suggested I look up an unnamed builder in a neighboring county whose shoddy construction practices could provide a wealth of material. Mike recalled that this individual managed to remodel a kitchen so badly that the refrigerator actually fell through the floor and into the basement in the middle of the night. The idiot contractor had notched the floor joists so some heat runs could be "buried" in the basement ceiling. Unfortunately, the heat runs were directly below the fridge. The unsuspecting homeowners were roused from their sleep in the middle of the night, certain a car had veered off the highway and into their home.

But a couple of calls to the building department failed to jog anyone's memory. Evidently his trail had gone cold. Yet bad contractors, like bad pennies, usually resurface over time, so I'm still hopeful this scoundrel will reappear.

Mike built new homes. I remodel old ones. One day he told me his idea of remodeling is to use a D-9. That's a bulldozer with a nine foot blade. This is fine, unless you're living in the home at the time, which Mike was.

The home he moved into was remodeled badly by a previous owner. (Pros can always spot an amateurish remodel.) The location of Mike's house was great and I know it looked nice enough to the casual observer.

But to the eye of someone like Mike, who had built high-end homes for many years, the funky texture on the ceilings, head-banging spiral stairs in the middle of the dining room, bad overall design, and vinyl siding just ate him up.

Self-remodeling. It's what we, remodelers, sometimes do to ourselves. Like self-abuse, self-immolation, and self-destruction, there comes a time when we must strap on our nail-belts at night and transform the building sins of the previous owners into something commodious and suitable for our own families.

One year, Mike did just that. He opened up the lower level of the two story, added a small bump-out to accommodate a new staircase, blew out a couple of walls, added a fireplace, remodeled the kitchen, installed new hardwood, and created a grand and luxuriant main floor.

He pulled it off without any disasters, but wasn't through yet. Lisa thought a bigger bathroom upstairs would be nice, and asked Mike is there was any way he could enlarge the hall bathroom. That winter he must have sat in his office scheming.

Realizing there was no way he could make the bathroom bigger without tearing off some of the roof, he made a bold decision. Never happy with the previous owner's "pop-top," which looked like a box dropped on one end of the house by a crane, he eliminated the entire second story, including both bedrooms. Mike's grand scheme ultimately added three bedrooms, three bathrooms, and walk-in closets to the new second story. The coup-de-grace to the old house was a spacious third floor game-room lounge.

Once begun, the project rolled along fine until the end of the second day.

The demo crew had managed to get half of the existing roof into the dumpster parked in the yard. This half was directly over the portion of the house Mike had remodeled the previous year. While the family vacated the premises and rented a small house conveniently located across the street, many of the furnishings were left on the new main floor area, since the garage was already filled. Thin plastic sheets protected their belongings from the nefarious dust.

The weather was clear and bright that morning – perfect for tearing off a roof. Unfortunately, "La Nina," ("El Nino's" wicked stepsister) decided the month of June was perfect for a protracted stay in our region. By the end of the day, shortly after the demo crew left, an ominous bank of clouds sneaked in from the west at dusk.

My house, around the corner, shook all night long from the ensuing lightning and thunder. I could only conjecture what the storm did to Mike's tarp.

The demo crew neglected to "pitch" the tarp before they left. All they did was securely fasten the edges of the tarp to the top of the outside walls. Just a couple of 2x 4's propped up in the middle would have stopped rainwater from collecting all night long...

The next morning, an eerie blue light flooded the upstairs. Over each bedroom hung a low blue ceiling filled with rainwater. Hundreds of gallons of agua sloshed precariously under the pinky dawn sky. The closet and hall walls helped support the suspended pools and keep the distended blue tarp off the floor.

One gallon of water weighs over six pounds; the collection in Mike's tarp may have weighed in at half a ton.

There was no neat and easy way to drain the tarps, but they eventually bailed out enough water from the top wall with ropes and buckets to reduce the volume enough to try to direct the flow over the top of the second story wall.

Maybe half of the water ran outside. The rest flooded the carpet, which was now a sponge.

Storms typically build up late in the afternoon, after a day of sunshine. When Mike's roof went into the dumpster, that all changed. The sky was turning purple by mid-morning. And an iridescent green tinge mingled in the darkening sky, signaling hail was imminent. The new tarp was only half up before the crew was contemptuously pelted with golf ball sized hail. They struggled mightily, but soon the winds and hail sent them to the shelter of their trucks. When the hail receded, they jumped back on the roof to construct a properly pitched tarp roof and shovel hail off the bedroom floor in what was now, mercifully, a shower.

It's difficult to work in the rain, especially from heights. Slips are common, and a bad one can cause a hospital stay. Power tools send jolts of varying degrees through limbs and trunks, quickly discouraging their use.

The new tarp was pitched, but conditions made it difficult and dangerous to continue. The crew had to pull off for the rest of the day.

The weather raged the second night too. Worse than the first. It was a good old-fashioned turd-floater.

The second story floor was a colander the next morning. Water rained through the ceiling. Giant paint blisters were everywhere. Drywall sagged and soggy strips of drywall tape trailed down like gloomy streamers. The new finishes Mike completed last year had acquired leprosy. Lisa opened her new kitchen cabinets and was drenched from waterfalls that gushed onto the countertops.

Furnishings stored on the main floor were ruined. Only a truck-sized "zip-loc" bag would have kept them dry. The new oak floor rippled and buckled. Every time Lisa attacked the water with a shop-vac, she got a bad shock.

The unseasonal rains continued for a week. Lisa bought the biggest tarp in the city – 40'x 60'. It took all summer for the house to dry out. The insurance settlement covered the water damages. Eventually, the new second story got built and shingled. The finished project is beautiful, and greatly adds to the comfort and value of his home. Was it worth it? I'm sure Mike spent more time off work and muttering to himself late nights than he bargained for. But that's the cost of "self-remodeling."

Psychotic Remodeling

18

DO YOU KNOW ME?
A MATCHING GAME

Match the Trade Professional with the Description

DESCRIPTION:

1. I'm known for the crack in my pants.
2. I make sure you fit in the "bulk plane."
3. Everyday I go to work with big suction cups.
4. I can evict you from your home.
5. Of all the tradesmen, my Workman's Compensation payments are the highest.
6. People who don't know me call me "Sparky."
7. I'm a CGR in the NAHB and NARI. This fall I'm going to the NRQA.
8. When I'm in a hurry, I heat my mud.
9. I can cut a bird's mouth.
10. I work with a CAD.

OCCUPATION:

a. Roofer
b. General Contractor
c. Building Inspector
d. Architect

e. Glazier

f. Drywaller

g. Zoning Official
h. Carpenter
i. Electrician
j. Plumber

See the next page for answers.

145

ANSWERS

1.**j** Plumber. "Junkies," "crack heads," and "drug addicts" may have crack in their pants, but they are not considered trade professionals.

2. **g** Zoning Official, not a Personal Fitness Trainer. The "bulk plane" is an invisible boundary that surrounds your property and extends above your roof. You can't hear it or feel it, but it's there. Too tall houses flunk the height restrictions.

3. **e** Glazier. The safest way to move large mirrors and pieces of glass is with large suction cups that provide adequate handles.

4. **c** Building Inspector. If work has been done and not properly permitted; if he feels a hazard may exist; if he considers the property unsafe; he can "red tag" or condemn your home on the spot and force you to leave.

5. **a** Roofer. Try to stand on a steeply pitched pitch roof 40 feet above the ground and you'll know why.

6. **i** Electrician. Traditional nickname. Electricians hate it.

7. **b** General Contractor. They love acronyms. He graduated from the **C**ertified **G**raduate **R**emodeler **P**rogram, and is a member of two national organizations: The **N**ational **A**ssociation of **H**ome **B**uilders, and **T**he **N**ational **A**ssociation of the **R**emodeling **I**ndustry. Every year, the **N**ational **R**emodelers **Q**uality **A**wards are presented.

8. **f** Drywaller. Chemical additives can make drywall joint compound (mud) harden quickly so that another coat can be applied in an hour instead of the next day.

9. **h** Carpenter. Not something a sadistic fiend would do. A "bird's mouth" is a notch in a roof rafter that helps it to set securely on the top of the wall.

10. **d** Architect. Not someone planning to a file a sexual harassment suit, a CAD is a **C**omputer **A**ssisted **D**esign system.

SCORE

10 correct. You're a long-time pro.

8-9 correct. You're in the business.

7 correct. You're ready to tackle a major remodel on your own.

6 correct. Better do some more research before "Doing It Yourself." (Contractors call Do-It-Yourselfer's DIY's.)

5 correct. Think about hiring a contractor and architect.

0-4 correct. You could care less

Help Wanted

Construction Superintendant

ESTABLISHED REMODELING firm seeks qualified and exp'd job site super-intendent for residential projects. Must co-ordinate all site activities from start to finish, including making sure no one gets hurt, shows up every day, and picks up after themselves. General babysitting duties req'd. Must have ability to respond to emergencies within 5 work-ing days. Ability to be in 3 places at once a plus. Tools, truck, min. 15 years exp. Computer skills, multi-lingual essential. Send resume to: S&M Construction, Box I-812, Loco, OK. 73442.

Construction Estimator

HOME BUILDER seeks applicant w/exp. in Project Management

19

COUCH POTATOES

At a loss to comprehend the mysteries of a home's construction, befuddled by the maze of wiring and pipes that run behind walls and seem to work 99% of the time, many homeowners overestimate the talents of remodelers and tradesmen skilled in the intricacies and nuances of how a house is put together.

The fact of the matter is, knowing how to install a dishwasher, for example, is no qualification for simple household tasks like setting up patio furniture, assembling toys, or even lugging a couch up some stairs.

Mike and Nancy F___, personal friends whose home I was in the habit of regularly visiting for minor repairs and improvements, asked me if I could help move their old couch up the back stairs and place it in the alley for the Salvation Army pickup scheduled for that afternoon.

Nancy left to do some shopping, and Mike and I were left to our own devices. Since we were handy around the house, we assumed moving the couch would be no problem. Although Mike didn't have a green thumb in the classic sense, I believe we were experimenting with a well-known weed shortly before we tackled the couch.

The finished ceiling in the basement was low, maybe just over seven feet. The hallways were narrow with corners everywhere. Fine for an adult male to walk around, but tight if you're a couch.

The couch was just out of the downstairs office and had barely turned the corner into the stairwell when we realized it was about six inches too long to turn the corner and make this task simple. It was too tall to stand on end and the corner was too sharp to navigate easily.

Operating under the logical (at that time) assumption that, "they got it down here somehow," we proceeded up the stairs as best we could, determined not to let a lifeless 180 lb. concoction of pine, upholstery, stuffing and springs get the best of us. Straightening the couch out halfway up the stairwell, the leg became wedged against the drywall just above the stair stringer. Ten or fifteen minutes of steady pushing, pulling, twisting and cursing did little to alleviate the dilemma. Exasperated, I launched one final desperate shove against the sofa and, amid the sound of drywall tearing and Mike being pushed squarely onto his buttocks as he held onto the couch, I jammed it permanently into the stairwell.

The good news was, it was an old couch. The bad news, it was about to become a love seat. I crawled beneath the wreckage I had created, grabbed my demo saw from the back of my truck, and soon was merrily sawing the couch in half.

I could hear Nancy's return over the drone of the saw, her musical voice wondering aloud if the couch was in the alley yet as she approached the back door. Seeing her expression as she turned and looked down the back stairwell was a pure Kodak moment. I'm sure she must have thought she was on "Candid Camera".

We spent another half-hour tearing through that tough old couch before it finally made its way out to the alley, destined for the trash man instead of the Salvation Army.

I made a few more trips to that stairwell during the week, patching and painting drywall. Good thing I was so handy.

FIXING A LEAK

A certain proficiency in minor plumbing and electrical work is required of most remodelers. Small contractors invariably fall under the designation, "Jack of All Trades." (This must have been the source of the pejorative, "All jacked up.") Sometimes the hardest part of a job is getting along with the people who hire you. They have to be cajoled and coddled, but also dealt with fairly, especially if most of your jobs come from word of mouth.

Some homeowners, however, would try the patience of Job, but at first I did not think Mrs. D___ was one of them. I remodeled her kitchen – new cabinets, countertops and fixtures. The job went smoothly, and I was done in three weeks. She began thinking of other work that needed to be done while I was there, and before long I was weatherstripping windows, regrouting bathroom tile, and replacing some soffit that was beginning to rot.

The day I finished she mentioned a laundry tub she had seen on sale at the local lumberyard, and the next day I was running a tee off the ABS drain in the basement. I finished early, checked the drains and supplies for leaks, and told her to phone me if she had any problems.

Two days later the call came. "Rick, there's a small leak under the downstairs sink." Drips are the bane of plumbers. It might take an hour of driving to tighten a nut a fraction, but I told her I'd swing by after work that day. Mrs. D___ wasn't too concerned about the drip – it was just "one of those things."

We walked down to the basement, and she showed me where she had seen the water. Sure enough, there was a dark spot at the bottom of the pipe where it ran out of the concrete floor. I flushed hot water through the sink, assuming I'd see the leak. Not a single drip. Then I slapped some tissue against the drain connections. They were dry as a bone. I put the wrench on all the connections, paying particular attention to the nut on the P-trap extension that ran into the tee. Nothing.

I turned on the upstairs water that was picked up by the drain; still no drips. I told her that sometimes, once a washer is saturated with water, it swells and then stops dripping. "All right," she said, "but if the leak reappears, I'll let you know."

Two days later, the phone rang at dinnertime. "It's wet again, and I wonder if you could come over to fix it."

That was the last thing I wanted to do at 6:00 in the evening, but I hoped one more trip might do it. When I got there I trudged downstairs and spotted a small puddle, about three inches around. I asked her if she had used the sink lately, and she claimed she had, about an hour before she called me. I reached down to touch the elusive fluid, and smeared it around in my fingers. Sure enough, water.

This time I was determined to get it. I turned all the water on full blast. She hovered nervously behind me as I crouched under the sink. Still no leaks. "Mrs. D___," I said, "I can't fix it if I can't see it. I'm sorry, but there's nothing I can do for you."

Tension crackled between us. Everything in her house was just so, and this would not do. From the look on her face, I could tell she was ready to call another plumber, have the drain and sink torn out, the floor jack hammered, and the resulting bill, for several hundred dollars, sent to me.

And then Misty, her old toy poodle, came to the rescue. Misty and I didn't get along too well. He yapped at me every morning, and I had to keep an eye on him after I caught the mutt chewing on my leather-wrapped hammer handle. He waddled down the stairs, gave me that patented "are-you-still-in-my-house?" look, and walked between us. Then he lifted his leg on the pipe, turned, and walked arrogantly upstairs.

I billed Mrs. D___ for two service calls.

She never paid for those service calls, but did send a couple of nice referrals my way as compensation.

21
THE
ROYAL FLUSH

Thomas Crapper is considered the spiritual Godfather of the modern flush toilet. It is unfortunate that the contributions of this Victorian-era plumber, buried in England's Elmer's End Cemetery since 1910, have been questioned of late by historical revisionists. Patent researchers now claim that they have been unable to piece together a paper trail fingering him as the inventor of the first flushing mechanism, although everyone concedes him his place in the annals of plumbing history.

His service to the Queen included plumbing over thirty lavatories with cedar wood seats to serve the regal bottoms in the 1880's. Despite the revisionists' conclusions, Crapper's reputation was forged through hard work, unabashed self-promotion, and incorporating the best technology available to serve the most high-end clients of his time. The famous plumber popularized the "syphonic flush" system in England, which released water from a tank high enough above the toilet bowl to ensure the veracity of the old proverb, that all (toilet bowl contents) must inevitably roll downhill.

Crapper was born in 1837, the same year Queen Victoria assumed the throne.

And in a weird twist, the 1846 Merriam-Webster's Collegiate Dictionary predates nine-year old Thomas' plumbing career with this prescient definition, where "to crap" means "to defecate." Oddly enough, in Britain the terms were never synonymous. Nevertheless, over the next century Thomas' surname and illustrious career plumbing the royal loos vaulted him into the Remodeler's Hall of Fame.

Crapper brought the outhouse indoors, an accomplishment that has touched us all. But the tale of progress hardly ends there.

A few years ago Toto Manufacturing introduced a toilet bowl seat that features more than just a hole in the middle. It is practically an appliance. It plugs into a wall outlet and is plumbed by a water line that branches off the toilet supply. A sensor tells this smart-seat when a backside is approaching and starts a small concealed electric fan that recirculates unpleasant air through a charcoal filter. 110 volts of electric current warms the seat against all those cold winter nights in a $40,000 bathroom and powers the washing mechanism.

The washing mechanism looks like a bent straw that emerges from a centerline beneath the seat. In the early models, it was controlled by a small remote device stored in a plastic bracket mounted on the wall alongside the paper holder. About the size of a VCR remote control, the system operates like a hand-held video game for preschoolers. An LCD screen depicts a playful seal. Press a button at the proper time, and the nozzle emerges. Press the "+" button, and the seal juggles one, two, and then three electronic beach balls. This denotes increased water pressure. Press the "-" button, the pressure decreases, and soon the seal is left with no balls.

Fortunately, the rinse water is warmed by an electrical element somewhere behind the nozzle, just like a "Bunn-O-Matic" coffee pot.

We put one of these attention-getters in a show home, covering the seat with clear carpet mask to allow gawkers an uninterrupted view of the ins and outs of this new product. It generated a lot of conversation, but not much in the way of sales.

I asked the eventual owners of the new home how they liked the high tech seat. Strictly professional curiosity. They hemmed and hawed a little bit before allowing only, "The children like to use it."

Now there is word that Matsushita, the Japanese electronics giant, is planning to market a space-age commode. Not only will it take your temperature, blood pressure, and weight, but it will analyze the urine of kidney and diabetes patients, and then transmit this data to the doctor!

I don't know what's next. Maybe a seat that speaks in English. Amateur researchers conclude that current models are believed to emit only high-pitched squeals and low rumbles, similar to the songs of humpback whales and other cetaceans.

I can't imagine that these high-end products would cause Mr. Crapper to turn over in his grave, but I believe that he would be inspired to sit up and take notice.

Psychotic Remodeling

22
SELF-
REMODELING

"A man's home is his castle," is an old cliche. I believe it's all right to invoke a cliche every now and then, especially one that holds so much truth.

Every person needs a sanctuary to escape the day's hassles, a place to feel safe. Sanctuaries come in many forms and guises, from a superstar's 60 room mansion to an immigrant laborer's bed. It's where we can toss our work faces in the front hall, flop on the couch, and nurture the soul as best we can.

Given an opportunity, we put our hearts and souls into these places, four walls and a roof. We dot our external landscape with family photos in an otherwise bare apartment, a crucifix on the wall opposite, or Grandma's antiques filling a 1920's flat. A suburban basement full of the flotsam left over from raising three kids, board games, bats and balls, special clothes and gifts. The clutter, to some of us, provides comfort. To others, it is a physical manifestation of haphazard thinking.

But no matter what surrounds us, when we sit at home in Grandpa's old wing back we can be ourselves.

Remodeling changes all that. When we come home to a place that looks like a bomb hit it (addition underway), or a tornado blew through (pop-top) or was flooded (leaky roof and plumbing disaster) it just gets hard to relax.

Your favorite chair is gone – in its place is a bucket collecting drips of rainwater. Every time you pick up a book or magazine, you know exactly where to return it because there is an outline in the dust that covers everything. Every morning, the framers manage to cut through the cable and phone wires that have been spliced back together the previous day. This offbeat dance of slicing and splicing has gone on for days. The framers give you the, "We're building a damn house, do we look like the freaking phone company?" look, and the job superintendent, the only human on the planet who is capable of fixing the phone line without a week's notice, won't be here for another hour, and he knows the first thing he'll do when he gets to work is fix the wires.

Look out the window. Your daily escape pod is free-falling into deep space. Experienced remodelers exercise care, caution, and concern with homeowners. They know, even if the homeowner doesn't, that there is a limited amount of goodwill they can draw from. The goodwill account usually gets close to overdrawn by the end of the job, but experienced remodelers know how to rebuild this account with a "freebie" here and there, by attention to detail (taking care of minor household crises, excessive tidiness, signing for packages, etc.) and really listening to a home-owner's concerns.

Opening up walls, tearing off roofs, and running through halls with a texture gun is akin to performing a triple by-pass on a human's heart and soul, minus the anesthetic. Hopefully, a little humor and perspective along the way can salve the inevitable wounds on the walls and psyche, because over time the two become hopelessly intermingled.

Heart surgeons don't operate on themselves. Even with assistance, it sounds like a bloody disaster. But remodelers do, and sometimes the results are gut-wrenching.

"It's perfect, we'll take it!" we told our first landlord. What we should have said was, "Hit us upside the head with 2x4's until we start making sense."

Country boys know how to do anything – fix a truck, roof a house, shoot a rifle, put up a fence, track a deer, run heavy machinery, and even perform crude surgery on livestock with techniques learned in 4-H.

I was a city boy and didn't know anything.

We were young and dumb, but didn't know it at the time. All Kathy and I knew was, we wanted to be together all the time. If this meant leaving a metropolitan area of 12 million people and moving 1,200 miles to a ghost town of 12 people, so be it.

We were standing in a six room house. The floor plan was exactly like half an egg carton, equal sized square rooms with an interconnecting doorway to each room. Every room had an exterior door except the bathroom. The southwestern house was an eighty year old adobe with a hip roof and a 4 & 12 pitch. Tires in neat rows on the west side held the new shingles down during the spring gales that roared through the valley. The house sat on a bluff thirty feet above the river, affording a clear view of the river and the Culebra Range beyond.

The only neighbors lived across the road and on the other side of the railroad tracks that bisected our property. Sheep ranches and alfalfa fields filled the bottom land. In the distance were old mining towns, their residents either ghosts or ancestors of the miners.

The house had been unoccupied for several years, except for the occasional chicken that sought shelter there. Feathers and droppings littered a couple of rooms. Unbeknownst to us at the time, the chicken theme would follow our lives like gum on the heel of a shoe. Many of the windows were broken, there was no water piped in the house, no cabinets, the "kitchen" ceiling was falling down. The heat consisted of one oil burning furnace in the middle of one room and a white coal-fired cook stove in the kitchen. It was...perfect!

We struck a deal with the landlord. If we helped get it habitable, we would get a break on the rent. Monthly rent: $35.

Henry M___ was our landlord. The descendant of Austrian immigrants who worked the mines at the turn of the century, his family businesses were a varied and sundry lot. His wife and mother ran the tavern on the highway. Behind the bar was the family kitchen (no door), the bedrooms beyond. They raised several kids and a couple of calves back there. Henry and his truck hauled coal up and down the river, and those of us with pickups could buy a front-end loader "scoop" for $25. In the sheds near the log-splitter hung Henry's private brand of jerky. Thin strips of venison and beef seasoned with hot or mild chilies dangled from the rafters. Of course, you had to take your chances with the black widow spiders when you went in there.

He had a few rental properties up and down the river, and today he was adding one more. He had picked this place up on the cheap and never gotten around to doing anything with it because he was always busy and, frankly, it wasn't a great market for re-habbing distressed properties. Henry was a good-looking man with square features and a well-proportioned, muscular build developed from a life of hard work. He usually wore a pocket T-shirt, and in his pocket was a hearing aid. The story was, Henry over-irrigated his own ears during a stint in the army and had about a 75% hearing loss. Being a frugal man, he never changed batteries until he was certain the old ones were completely drained. Consequently, Henry was a very good lip reader and his friends were very hoarse. When he eventually changed batteries, it was obvious not because Henry seemed to understand what was being said, but because the feedback was terrible and this box about the size of a pack of cigarettes would squawk and whine from the front of his chest. Funny thing was, every time Henry was around his wife and her endless lists, his batteries were suddenly dead. He'd point to his shirt pocket, mumble a few words, and shake his head. When we'd catch him talking to Annette this way, he'd wink when she wasn't looking. Annette rolled her eyes when Henry wasn't looking.

Looking back, the genesis of my remodeling career can be traced to the moment I struck a bargain with Henry. He asked if I knew anything about plumbing and drywall, and I answered, "uh-uh," which I took to be a negative response. Henry, owing to his hearing condition, thought I responded in the affirmative – "uh-huh," and the next day we began transforming a hovel into a home.

"Jim" F___ and Henry did the lion's share of getting "Chez-Poulet" back together. I was the laborer. City water had been piped into the cellar below the kitchen and future bathroom years before; now it was just a matter of piping the fixtures from below. We made a great team, Henry and I. Henry worked upstairs and I was down in the cellar, feeding him pipes. He couldn't hear anything I said and I didn't know a coupling from a nipple. Kathy spent a lot of time ferrying instructions between the two of us, running outside and then downstairs, and then back up as I shoved pipes through the floor and Henry connected the lines. I had no idea what I was doing, but eventually the water began running.

The house was bare, so when we needed large ticket items like water heaters and propane stoves, we went to Henry's barn. This is 25 years before the concept of a "Big Box" store. Henry's barn was in many ways superior, and legendary in the valley for what it held.

Old barns devoid of livestock have a mausoleumesque quality. The walls were cinder block, and it had a huge mansard roof with siding under the gables. As far as barns go, it was a classic model. Henry kept two Kaisers in mint condition, a '52 and a '53, inside under wraps. Wood stoves, gas stoves, rows of sinks and fittings, toilets, water heaters, truck parts, auto body parts, hardware, horse shoes, farm implements, plows, chain saws, hand tools, jacks and tires, refrigerators, freezers, furniture, signs, windows, and doors were stacked and tucked away on the dusty, straw strewn floor. The aisles meandered like a river around the big stuff, the cars and truck beds. Little side canyons led up to mountains of buckets filled with bolts or dead-ended against undefinable rusty machinery. Dust hung thick in the air. Light filtered through the cob-webbed windows and missing boards in the gable ends; pigeons flapped in the darkness above. A curtain of logging chains hung in one corner, clanking like eerie wind chimes.

Just up the hill from Henry's barn were the remnants of the mining town. Maybe all that was left of the lives of its citizens had made its way to his barn, as if Henry was the caretaker by default of relics of a town long disappeared. The company buildings had been razed 60 years earlier, the foundations filled in by dust storms.

Mostly dead trees stood in rows, marking where front yards used to be. Hands of greenery still clung to some trees, waving in the spring breeze.

I helped Henry wiggle stoves out from against the wall as he tried to find the one pictured in his mind. We looked behind them for fittings, checked for burners and grates, and eventually came up with a monstrous old white propane stove from the 1940's. We loaded it onto the flatbed truck along with a Montgomery Wards steel sink cabinet, a 6 foot integral cast sink and countertop with drainboard, and then slowly followed the bumpy road to the little house down the river, below the tipple.

"Jim" F___, who we knew from the Big City, was a great help transforming "Chez Poulet" into "Chez MacKay." The fact that we were crashing at his home for a couple months provided extra motivation. He lived in Henry's "mansion" on the other end of town at the bottom of a small bridge that spanned a dry wash gully. He got me started glazing windows and drywalling ceilings, indispensable skills for my next incarnation. "Jim" revealed to me the mysteries of filling the joints between the drywall sheets with perforated tape and drywall mud, and how continuous applications of drywall mud would eventually cause the ceiling to look like one piece – what a concept!

Later instead of sooner we were ready for paint. Only two rooms out of the six needed it right away, the kitchen and bathroom. Henry had a lot of paint in his barn but the only colors were yellow and white. The white was the same as the dotted line in the middle of the highway, and the yellow was the yellow of the no passing lane because Henry got a great buy on paint from the highway department. Kathy vetoed the yellow, which was the color the walls already were. But we figured the paint would stand up to anything and had to be easy to clean (if it could withstand hail storms and road kill then it had to be perfect for a kitchen) so we bought some tint for the white paint and came up with a creamy coffee color for the walls, leaving the ceiling white.

The night we painted the ceiling still burns in my mind. We ate an early dinner, then cleared the big oak table, chairs, and sofa out of the kitchen and put them on the wraparound porch. Plastic covered the 1940's style linoleum tile, and we rolled the ceiling in record time. The paint smelled pretty bad but covered in one coat. When we started the walls we made sure all the windows and doors were opened. It was a clear night and the stereo was blasting "Tommy" by The Who. The more we painted, rolling the walls, the worse the coverage seemed to get. Our jaws dropped, turned slack, and instead of long sweeping rolls that covered the most square footage possible, we were making little baby rolls up and down, working over the same square foot of wall for what seemed like an eternity. The texture on the walls kept swirling and moving, making it that much more difficult to get good coverage. At the same instant, we turned to look at each other. I was as shocked by Kathy's dopey-looking glazed-over "what are we on?" look as she was by mine although, to be quite candid, that look was not the stranger to my face that it was to hers.

"I think it's the paint," was about all I could say as the inside of my head seemed to swell and float, exactly like a helium balloon full of mushy brains. The top of my head soared off and bounced against the ceiling, bobbing in time to the music. We dropped our rollers in the pans and stumbled outside as if chased by demons, trying to suck in the cool blue mountain air and rinse our brain cells of the toxic chemicals we had inhaled. The fumes hit us both at once, after about thirty minutes of exposure. We stumbled half a mile down the tracks to the old UMWA hall and spent the night, hoping we'd be normal when we woke up.

Although somewhat addled the next day, our misery was reduced to the level of a mid-range hangover. We went out for breakfast, got some fans to move the fumes out, and finished the job up as quickly as we could with minimal brain damage. Now I know why they paint highways outside. Whew!

Our college experiences didn't translate into useful and income-producing endeavors in this nether-land, so I enrolled in the local junior college and finished the building trades program. I learned how to read a framing square, build a house, and, after some practice, not poke myself in the groin with the shaft end of a rigging ax when I hammered walls together. Before I knew it, I was gutting out complete houses and reassembling them as cheap rentals. I think the appeal of remodeling was my core belief that no matter how nice the home or no matter where the location, it would always be in need of repair and I could always make a living fixing up someone's house somewhere.

There's something about living in a ghost town surrounded by other ghost towns full of desperate people with limited opportunities who think the outside world is weird that eventually eclipses the inherent natural beauties and solitude that surrounded us. It was time to move on.

I found an old mink ranch on the outskirts of a major metropolitan area. The structure was two cinder block houses joined in the middle by a garage. The single story on the south side was occupied, but the two story on the north was for rent only for several hours before I snapped it up. It sat on three acres in the middle of the landlord's 100 acres of pasture with a long and low outbuilding in the back, formerly a kennel, full of little 4'x 6' cages. This large outbuilding was the ideal place to house my tools and equipment. The cages helped organize my various woodworking projects. The unfinished table in one cage, the unfinished rocker in another cage; it made a great shop.

The only problem with the house was that it was too small. The upper level was finished, but it was only one bedroom, and Kathy and I were ready to start a family. The lower level was bare. It needed a remodeler's touch.

The landlord wondered who these new tenants were, who liked to fix up his property for free. But the nesting urge hit hard and drove us to strike a deal: He supplied the materials and we supplied the labor.

Minks aren't raised because they provide milk or eggs. Their gift is not quite as neat and tidy. This old mink ranch had a cooler for pelts in the lower level. It was an insulated plywood room, about 9'x 11', the perfect size for a child's bedroom. Of course, the compressor would have to go. So too would the six inch thick meat locker style door with the chrome commercial latch on the outside and push knob release on the inside. As a matter of fact, we took the entire wall out, paneled the room with left over cedar siding, added carpet and track lighting, and had a cozy and quiet little baby room for Travis.

The rest of the basement was taken up with a family room and laundry facilities, and was quite serviceable until another basic human urge sent us packing.

It was time to buy a house. There was enough money left over from Kathy's father's estate for a down payment, so we took this gift and went shopping for over a year until we finally found the – well, it wasn't the perfect place, but we were secure in the knowledge we had done the best we could.

The houses in our price range were borderline dumps. We knew if we were patient and kept looking the right house for us would eventually turn up. We looked in the mountains – too far from work and too cold. We looked in the suburbs – too much of that bland sameness of housing and humans. We combed through some of the older and closer-in suburbs, but nothing seemed to be available. Finally, after over a year of searching, we put a contract on a house in the city.

The house certainly met first-time home buyer's criteria. It was one of the worst houses in a nice neighborhood. The neighborhood, in fact, was reminiscent of the area we grew up in. There were many large homes, tree-canopied streets, parks, shopping, schools, and a nearby university helped anchor the neighborhood. The elementary school was half a block down the street, and Travis was ready for kindergarten. In a summertime ritual, we discovered bats flew out from under the clay tiled elementary school roof at dusk to flit up and down the street.

There was an eclectic blend of people – college kids, old and young couples, big families and singles who all shared an area defined by natural boundaries and the absence of thru streets to help create a quiet enclave in the city.

Kathy loved the house, and that carried a lot of weight. I had my doubts about the structure – some of the design was unconventional. But I loved the area, was sick of looking, and knew a fixer-upper was our best bet. After all, it was time we fixed up our own place and not the landlord's.

This place was about 800 square feet. It was a one story ranch with a decent sized living room in front, a large galley kitchen with an adequate eating space area past it, and two bedrooms, a bathroom, and a hallway in the back.

Five large box-elder trees along the south fence shaded the house in the summer. The box elder, to some, is a hideous tree. In many jurisdictions they are illegal, although Mother Nature has never been personally issued a citation. Arborists believe their weak wood is prone to disease and attracts bugs. The specimens outside my windows have great twisted black burled trunks with numerous crotches for tree houses and handholds for children. The bark has fallen off the upper reaches of the trees' desiccated limbs, revealing almost silvery deadwood that provides nesting and shelter for countless birds. Industrious ladderback woodpeckers crawl their limbs, pecking, searching for bugs. Flickers, the Remodelers of the Bird World, peck two inch holes in dead limbs to create shelter for other species. One hole at the end of a hollowed-out limb has been an annual nest for fifteen consecutive years to starlings.

When one branch is pruned a dozen replace it, like the heads of the mythological Hydra. The little suckers require constant trimming. Left unattended, the new branches sprout in all directions. On nights in the dead of winter I study their naked misshapen limbs, now set against the background of a cobalt and ash sky, from the warmth of my hot tub below. I feel like I am in a Tim Burton movie.

The front yard of this awkward little home had a beautiful black locust and a blue spruce. But a couple of the walls were a little too out of plumb, the foundation wasn't typical of a home of that era, there were some puzzling over-framing details in the attic, and the siding was a hideous mustard-yellow asphalt shingle.

The perceived size of the interior shrank by 50% as soon as we moved our furniture in, and we felt like we lived in a storage locker. Looking around at the big dark furniture, we felt really cooped up. The neighborly couple across the street, the new residents on the block, came over and introduced themselves. They had lived in the same house for fifty years. Warren H___ was tall and rail-thin, with scraggly gray hair and a pointed beard. His dentures seemed to be one size too big and clicked and clacked when he talked. Owing to the fact he worked graveyard all his life, he could never adjust to sleeping nights. He slept days and had a ghostly pallor because of it. His wife was very sweet, and worked in her garden and created baked goods all day. Their house started out small and over the years Warren added on to it until it was a nicely done 2,200 square foot tri-level.

I looked at them and wondered if this was our future selves come to pay a visit.

Unfortunately, they had something else on their minds.

"Should we tell them, Gracie?" Warren asked with a wicked gleam in his eye.

Tell us what?

"Oh, Warren, they just moved in."

The place is haunted, we were thinking.

"Well, I think they should know," Warren stated matter-of-factly.

We had just sunk every penny we had into this place. We smiled weakly but with great curiosity. "Now you have to tell us," Kathy said.

"Well, this place used to be two chicken coops. After World War II they put them together and made a house."

Shades of Chez Poulet!

Evidently Warren always took great delight in this little revelation. I had a feeling he told this to all the residents at this address. Seeing our shocked expressions, Grace tried to smooth things over a little, and added, "The house next door used to be the barn. When we bought our place it was the farmhouse. It was just tiny. Warren's done so much..."

I don't know how many additions I have built. If I were to sit down and make a list, I suspect I could come up with around fifty. They all had one thing in common. They were called *additions*.

For the longest time, the one in our back yard was called "The Hole."

Not long after we moved in, I was industriously making improvements to the small house. I added lights in the crawl space, extra insulation, caulked the windows, installed a huge skylight in the bathroom on the north side, and improved the landscaping. I closed in the back porch to add a badly needed laundry room. The whole time, I thought and measured and planned how the addition we were going to put in the back one day would look. I ordered extra trim on my trim jobs and stockpiled it. I saved extra 2"x 12"x 20's and incorporated them into the design. I had more salvage than a junkyard: Atrium doors, cast-iron steeping tubs, metal clad windows, light fixtures, a furnace, a hot water-heater, and a near-new toilet, all went into the design. I salvaged oak flooring and quarter sawn oak for the vanity from all of the high-end remodels I was doing. I bought custom skylights from the plastics supplier that were discounted 50% only because the size was wrong. I incorporated salvaged fixtures, doors, and mirrors from "The Lanai" into the design. Over the years, I stockpiled matching hardware. My final hardware bill was zero. Materials and parts were tucked into every nook and cranny of the little house. Cleaning out an old storehouse, I hauled off enough carpet and tile for my floor finish. Before I began, my garage looked like Henry's barn.

The only thing I didn't have was money. It was the era of gas lines and double digit inflation. We tried to refinance, but the housing market was depressed. Some appraisers calculated that our home actually lost value.

In slow times, home builders move into the remodel market and that nearly doubles the competition. Remodelers were doing any and every job they could find to keep their businesses alive. I was struggling, and falling behind with my bills – even the mortgage had a couple of 0-30 days late postings. We needed a 90% loan-to-value to put the deal together, and my credit rating at that time was approaching the high-risk category. I didn't tell Kathy about the late payments, so as our financial history unfolded under the scrutiny of the bankers and underwriters, more strains developed in our marriage. Just when we needed to be strong together, things between us were unraveling. We eventually put together enough money to get started. I projected that we could get into framing with our meager funds.

This madness was fueled by the fact that Kathy was due with our second child right around Christmas, and we were breaking ground in September...

Before I broke ground, I was making two critical mistakes. Not having enough cash to keep the construction train fueled was one mistake, and the second was setting a deadline that I couldn't possibly meet. I drew up a set of plans that incorporated all of the house parts I had and would be simple enough for one man to assemble. We were adding on a family room that opened up off the back of the house, and then a stairwell going to the upstairs master bedroom and two bedrooms in the garden level downstairs. Below the family room was a large mechanical closet. We were adding over 900 square feet of living space to the house. Very little of the work was sub-contracted. Only forty hours was subbed out during the entire project. I hired a plumber to help me with the underground drains, an electrician to set the meter, concrete finishers for the flat work, carpet layers for the bedrooms and stairs, and floor finishers for the oak.

Another problem was twofold: There wasn't enough time in the day and there was only one of me. Besides working weekends and evenings, laying up brick in the middle of the night under the glare of 300 watt bulbs, I was pulling off of paying jobs to keep the addition going. This reduced the cash flow at a time I needed it most. We got a personal loan from Chris L___, a close friend to whom we'll be eternally grateful.

Another dark haired woman entered my life about this time. She worked in a clinic at the Medical Center, helping families – expand. Ms. A___ lobbied me to enlist in the program usually advertised in the back of the classifieds with the "Safe Sex, Get Paid!" come on.

She suggested I become a sperm donor.

The next week I filled out the questionnaire and somehow convinced the office manager that their was no evident history of mental illness in my family. Soon, after minimal effort and no formal training, I was collecting $35 a day for something I used to do for free. I must admit I managed some satisfaction from helping other families with their own "additions." Every day that I dropped off the goods in the hospital's mail room, I left the facility making a mental note that I had done just enough hard time to purchase a square of shingles or the drywall for one room.

After a few months, however, I began to lose enthusiasm and the frequency of my deposits began to taper off. At that time in my life I was not considered a morning person and the freezer doors shut by 9:30 AM. Soon, I found I was sweating deadlines.

But I think the special deliveries were what finally did me in.

I would get clandestine calls to be in a specific parking garage at 6:45 PM (I felt like "Deep Throat") with the goods. Then, I was to take the service elevator to the third floor. Although the office would be dark and seem closed, the implication was that there was an ovulating woman and her husband in a room down the hall.

One day I was early and the couple was late, so the three of us shared a service elevator on the way to the third floor, my tell-tale brown baggie in hand. Instead of setting it on the front counter like I was instructed, I should have just handed them the stupid thing and offered my premature congratulations...

Our daughter, Clarity, was born around Christmas. The addition didn't even have a subfloor. When she arrived in the world all we had completed to date was a four foot deep foundation wall, some rough plumbing, and some backfill.

Over the next two years I worked nights and weekends, and took a couple of weeks off here and there to side the house or hang the drywall. I wired the house with romex salvaged from another job. By the time the inspector got around to signing off on it, the wire itself was outdated and I had to rewire the whole addition – with romex I paid cash for!

Travis' ninth birthday was celebrated in the addition. We hung crepe paper from the trusses, I covered the safety rail around the stairwell with scrap plywood, and we stapled balloons to the bare studs. It was nice having so much extra room, and we looked forward to the day we could actually use it like a normal family. At least we called it an addition now, instead of "The Hole."

Clarity was a toddler by the time the addition was close to completion. Her mother was exhausted at night from working on film and video projects, and many times the tables were turned with the three year old putting her mother to bed. Then Clarity pulled on some rubber galoshes to protect her feet, and walked out the back door of the house and through the addition door to visit me as I ran trim or installed fixtures after dark. She pulled up a little plastic chair we kept in there for her and we'd talk about her day while she watched Daddy work to exhaustion.

The new mechanical closet was the lowest level of the house and the lowest level of my building life. It was home for the sump pit, furnace, and water heater. The main sewer drain bisected it at chest level. When it was time to hook up the furnace I couldn't fit the big cold air returns around the sewer drain. I struggled all day. The only option was to take the cast drains apart, a job I wanted to avoid at all costs. I was so exhausted and frustrated the weight of the whole project just hit me at once and I broke down. (If I'd been thinking clearly, I would have disassembled the drain from the outset and saved several hours of misery.)

The Hole has been finished for many years and turned out to be wonderful, although the kids wish it were bigger. I never had one drywall crack or nail pop. I attribute that to the fact that the framing lumber was completely dry and well-seasoned for over a year before the drywall went up. Taking Mr. Wright's advice, I planted ivy on the north side.

I used every trick I knew to build it for $15 a square foot. Even at that time, it was an impossibly low price.

Making over my own home, doing it to myself, caused as many internal changes to my psyche and internal well-being as the obvious physical changes to the property. It was something I didn't expect. Much of it was painful, but as we all know, good things sometimes hurt.

There's just one thing.

Addition floors "plane" out to match the existing level unless unusual circumstances dictate otherwise. This addition entry is a 3 foot wide arched opening with a one and one half inch step. I finished it the best I could. I bullnosed the oak and hung it out some to create a shadow line to make it more visible. Bugs hide under it and people trip over it. I must have thought I was going to add an extra sill plate to the sub-floor or planned on using 2x8's instead of 2x6's. We call it "The Tripper," and it is a source of acute embarrassment to me. But since three and a half years eclipsed between the time I poured the foundation it sits on and I installed the last board, I'll write it off to "unusual circumstances."

Building for myself is different than building for others. (Actually, I started and finished a couple of additions in my professional life as my personal hell dragged on in the back yard.) It's a more organic process. I consult the plans as I've drawn them so that concrete and framing will fit together, and then the plans are stuck on a high shelf to collect dust. During construction I stare at a blank wall, maybe picturing what shelving will look like that is appropriate for my particular needs. Kathy knows that look, when I stare a certain way, visualizing another household project. She'll always ask, "What is it? What are you planning now?" This look is distinct from when I am staring blankly without the benefit of thought.

Some remodel jobs allow me the luxury of working this way. Some entrances require arches, others need an angular or a molded frame. Some rooms are round and curvy, others are square. Traffic patterns, textures, lighting, furnishings and more subliminal effects all need to be evaluated as a craftsman turns something out of the back of a truck into a home.

I collect souvenirs from my jobs. Two fire brick from the huge palace in the pines are in my front door stoop, distinguished from the others by their blonde characteristics. I collected a brick from our first home, the old adobe, long after it burned to the ground one clear arctic night, and laid it in the wall by the Atrium door in our addition. Our best kitchen knife is an old skinning knife I found in the ruins of a dilapidated shed a mile into the chaparral from where I built my first addition. My hands and arms are dotted with small scars. Sometimes I wonder if there are scars on my heart.

There is a sameness to many of the old villages nestled in the valleys of Europe. Seen from afar, the tile roofs and stucco walls have a consistent hue, their elements probably mined from the same mountainside to create an architectural uniformity over the centuries unlike anything found in garish America. The stucco and tile hues of every village vary from region to region, just like the earth the finishes were pulled from.

In a different way, my addition reflects the urban landscape it was built in. I pulled it out of the back alleys and tract developments, salvaging 40 year old doors from the trash that happened to match mine; collecting brick after brick from the weeds and alleys, from old houses around the corner that I or another builder had torn up or torn down. The collection of brown and red-hued bricks gave rise to the moniker, "University Blend," as other builders mimicked my salvage efforts.

I asked "Jim" F___, when he was a bricklayer, how a 500 foot brick smokestack was built. Thinking of scaffolding, the heights, weather, and the sheer enormity of the project, it seemed like an almost impossible task to me. He explained the art of masonry very simply: "It's one on top of two."

I write the same way I build. The finished project is pictured in my mind. I'll collect scenes and phrases, and quirky words, and tuck them away in one of a multitude of vacant brain cells or in notebooks, knowing the right place for them will eventually be revealed. (I'm still looking for a place for the word, "grist.") Eventually, I collect enough bits and pieces to fashion into walls constructed from memories.

Psychotic Remodeling

23 FINISHED!!

Before your new project is finished it will begin to fall apart.

Not because of faulty workmanship or defective materials, but because a home is a constant maintenance item.

Homeowners aren't aware that their home, although not a biological-ly-based consciousness, is actually a moving, breathing thing. Soffits and attics require ventilation to circulate air so moisture does not become trapped in walls and cause wood damage. Crawl spaces, appliances, and fixtures require ventilation also. Hardwood floors need gaps around their perimeters (covered by baseboards) to allow for seasonal expansion and contraction. Great expanses of stucco and concrete need control joints to accommodate the inevitable shrinkage. Exterior walls need vapor barriers to stifle the moisture-laden outside air that naturally moves to the interior of the home. Dissimilar materials that expand and contract at different rates (ceramic tile and wood, for example) require caulk joints to mitigate cracking between the two. Modern homes that are relatively air-tight require outside air for ventilation.

Minor settling will occur in almost any home built of wood, and in dry climates lumber and hardwood floors will shrink. In humid climates doors stick and floors that have not been allowed to expand will cup. A slight gap or a tear in the caulk between a counter top and the side splash, for example, has happened because the lumber in the floor has settled from shrinkage or deflection. The new side splash has stayed on the wall, the counter has dropped, and the caulk between them has torn.

Drywall corners and joints crack out because of shrinkage behind the walls and settling above doors and windows. Screws and nails "pop" when this happens.

Finished flooring, like oak, develops gaps between the planks in arid climates because of these common processes. Weatherstripping is scuffed, scratched, and split. Spots of rust appear on iron balconies and fret work.

Naturally occurring salts in masonry are nourished by moisture retained in the wall. Over time white patches bleed through to the outside veneer. This harmless "New Building Bloom" is called "efflorescence," and eventually disappears.

Hard water creates deposits in new plumbing fixtures, leaving brown scaly rings that even Mr. Tidy Bowl can't remove. Sacrificial anode rods in water heaters are designed to attract corrosive minerals instead of the permanently installed tank lining. These anodes should be replaced after several years. Few homeowners know this is a maintenance item. And seldom used shut-off valves should be opened and closed twice a year, just to give the valve a little exercise. Owners of old homes that have to deal with a corroded shut-off valve for minor repairs (new washers, etc.) can find themselves in Mississippi Man territory if the main valve busts. Don't forget – most plumbing corrodes from the "inside out." This means the pipe or fixture may look fine on the outside and not fall apart until a wrench touches it.

In humid climates, wood doors and windows swell and stick. Sea air and exterior paint are always at odds in coastal climates.

The slightest bit of uneven tension on a standard door hinge can cause a squeak the week after the last carpenter walks out the door.

If your addition is finished in the fall, gutters will collect leaf debris if there are no gutter guards. Over time, this debris turns into an organic sludge mixed with fresh granules that have already washed off your new shingles. Gutters and downspouts can become clogged with this vile mixture. When that happens, water backs up and tries to enter your home. Airborne seeds actually sprout in the spring from neglected gutters, turning them into planters.

The stuff in your gutters is strawberry cheesecake compared to what collects in your drains. Plumbing traps are a maintenance item for every household that washes or shaves their hair. Inordinate amounts of congealed gunk accumulate in sewer lines that aren't pitched properly or have too-tight bends in them. Like plaque and cholesterol in a heart patient's arteries, too much of a bad thing in a home's drains is a recipe for disaster. Sewer rats (plumber's jargon for discarded feminine hygiene products) tend to congregate in these bad places deep in your home's bowels. Over time, things back up.

Tree roots seek out these sewer lines for sustenance, and then clog the line that feeds them.

Anal retentive homeowners concerned about the condition of their home's innards can view sewer drain interiors through the aid of a small TV camera on the end a cable. Not for the faint of heart, this hi-tech device displays unsolved mysteries on a small black and white monitor.

Ultra-violet radiation affects buildings in high altitudes. Paint, exterior finishes, and even carpet fades more quickly when it is exposed to high UV sunlight.

Airborne bacteria clings to the grout in your new tiled bathroom. Like an infection, it can spread if the conditions are ripe. Mold likes moisture and darkness. Fans, sunlight, and disinfectant are necessary to prevent mildew from discoloring grout and caulk, and spreading to other areas of the building where it can ruin clothes, cause respiratory infections in family members, and inflict structural damage. There are over 100 different varieties of mold that can be found in the average household. Many of them can cause allergic reactions in susceptible homeowners – and some, over time, are deadly.

Homes in the country will be reclaimed by the wildlife. Woodpeckers create holes in foam-backed synthetic stucco to build safe nests in unreachable places. Swallows build mud nests on the synthetic stucco wall you insisted the stucco guy redo twice. Other birds will build more conventional nests in exterior nooks and crannies, and many insects will find your expensive lumber – delectable. Bats find the spaces under clay roof tiles are acceptable substitutes for a cave. Foul-smelling and four-legged mammals will seek the sanctuary of a low porch deck. Raccoons have crawled down chimneys to breed. Small rodents scurry inside for the winter as soon as the leaves turn color.

Dead bugs have migrated like lemmings to the crevices in the window seals. Their lifeless husks need to be wiped away periodically to ensure tight seals against the elements. Scientists estimate that 90% of the dust in our homes is composed of these mummified bug casings, sloughed-off human skin cells, and hair that has been shed by all species of household inhabitants. Monster-Vacs need to probe and suck clean a home's duct system every decade or so to remove these nests of filth as they accumulate. Properly installed air filters that guard us from these hazards must be replaced regularly.

Concrete sitting on improperly tamped soil will drop in the first year. Some of the items installed in your home by well-meaning tradesmen will be defective. Faucets, toilets, switches and appliances may all develop glitches. One client was understandably annoyed when the new garage door decided to go up and down in the middle of the night for no apparent reason.

When a contractor completes a major remodel for a homeowner, a "walk-thru" is scheduled around the end of the job. Homeowners needn't waste time making more than informal judgments on unacceptable items before the walk-thru. If the contractor and the homeowner have been utilizing good communication skills throughout the job there will be few surprises during the walk-thru. A good contractor knows all of the little things that need to be straightened out before the walk-thru better than any homeowner. All of the vested parties "walk-thru" the project together and compile lists to organize any remaining work. These lists contain items that were not completed or were completed unsatisfactorily. Homeowners also include items they want performed at an additional or no cost.

These lists are called punch lists.

Fresh carpet seams that have not yet laid down are always on the punch lists. Invariably, painters leave masking around windows and behind doors. Sometimes they leave overspray on hinges and weather-stripping. Doorknobs may be loose. Rough spots in the drywall finish or paint may be present. It is not unusual for laminate countertops to have sharp edges or nicks that need attention. Splattered cement always makes the list. In one show home, the shower didn't drain. The homeowners feared the worst. But the plumber had merely forgotten to remove the test plug, a thin plastic membrane located a few inches down the drain.

Some homeowners who have spent lots money (i.e. way over budget) get persnickety at the end of a job and find fault with everything. I know for a fact that some owners crawl around on their hands and knees, their snouts inches from the floor, and poke their heads into strange spaces at unusual angles to find a speck of dust painted over on a piece of trim so that they will have a comprehensive punch list. I know this because I have to contort my body like an Indian Yogi to correct the problem.

A lurking fear has begun to grow in the hearts of these owners. Soon, the carpenters and painters will forever leave their home. Their last opportunity to have corrections made is at hand – if hardware isn't tightened and trim touched up NOW it will never happen. These owners, before long, forget about the 99.8% of the project that is wonderful and worry that the floor will squeak in four months. *What happens then?*

These owners must understand that a home or remodel job *will never be perfect.*

Wood has knots and splinters, and tile has variations in color and size. Small pits and bumps can be found in the finishes of most ceramic and porcelain products. Builder's groups estimate there are over 3,000 parts in a typical home. Some of these items are produced by slave laborers in Third World Countries. How can everything be perfect? Some homeowners expect their finished architectural product will fit together like a finely engineered Swiss watch – sleek, polished, and on time. What these owners fail to realize is that little spots and blemishes in the overall finish effectively disappear when furnishings are added. Like a beautiful woman with a temperamental complexion, she just needs some makeup and accessories to knock the socks off any admirer. Novice homeowners spend too much time obsessing about the pimples.

A walk-thru is also an opportunity for homeowners and contractors to review basic operating procedures for furnaces, motion detectors, and any other appliances or home systems that require instruction.

If the project is on schedule, the punchlist may be very long. If it has dragged on interminably, waiting for parts to dribble in, the contractor may have taken care of a lot of items that would have otherwise made the list. Before the walk-thru, the contractor should have taken care of everything possible. In a perfect world the only items left undone should be on backorder.

(I saved the most extensive list from my "new home-repair-warranty-punchlist" career. It has eleven pages and 217 separate items. Some were simple, like "sweep garage floor," and "clean paint off transformer." Other items were more involved, like tearing out twelve concrete steps from the eight foot wide staircase that approached the front door – the riser heights were inconsistent – to painting the pond gravel. In this particular residence, some "flat liners" had sanded errant paint flecks off the expensive touch-sensitive dimmer switches, ruining every one. In all fairness, the house was monstrous. My home at that time would have probably fit in this house's "Great Room." And the pond with the unpainted gravel – half of it was in the entry, the other half was in the back yard. I'm sure the owners moved in on schedule, though.)

The punch list is usually compiled room-by-room, with the exterior portion of the house a separate category.

When the list is as complete as possible, it's time to sort through the items at a meeting. Hardware that is on back-order should not affect the closing or final payment. The best tactic is to not pay for items that are not completed, from towel bars to patio slabs. Items that can be corrected (clean-up items and bad trim, for example) should be taken care of ASAP by the contractor. In most cases, the contractor really wants to finish before the client moves into the space because his job is twice as tough when the area is lived in. He has to be tidier, so he spends more time being neat and cleaning up after himself, and less time is spent on actual construction items. Working time is sometimes brought to a standstill as he tries to accommodate plumbing repairs around the family's schedule.

Many of the items that have made the punch list because they were not entirely completed are there for a reason other than there wasn't enough time in the day. A little item, "switch plate is crooked," can be a harbinger of extensive surgery. The plate is crooked because the box in the wall is not set correctly. A repair may involve opening a hole in the wall, fiddling with the electrical box, and the ensuing patching, texturing, and painting.

Also, the owner dings up walls and doors during the long-anticipated move-in, creating more work not in the contract. Most decent contractors go ahead and fix the dinky stuff and throw in a few freebies here and there because he knows there are other items on the punch list he can't repair to everyone's satisfaction.

Synthetic stucco is difficult to repair. A small bit of troweling rarely matches the original finish. If the application was more than a few weeks apart, the colors dry at different rates, and patches and touch-ups can look worse than the original problem.

If there is a small defect in a large stucco wall, it may be unrealistic to ask your contractor to re-trowel the entire wall to fix small a blemish on the side of the house. If you are a homeowner who is genuinely pleased with the total finished product except for a few things here and there, the homeowner has an opportunity to be a negotiator instead of a jerk. If the contractor feels he is on the hook for the entire wall and doesn't want to do it, know what you want in return. Maybe a less than perfect patch in an out of the way place and some credit on the final bill will make everyone happy.

A critical question homeowners should pose to the contractor's references is this: "How would you describe the service your contractor provided after the project was completed?" No customer will ever forget lousy service.

If the project is small, like a carport, and built correctly in the first place, there is probably no need for a return trip or service call. An extensive project, like a kitchen or addition, usually requires one or two regularly scheduled service calls. Problems that are safety and security issues should be dealt with promptly. Exterior doors and windows that won't close, badly leaking roofs or plumbing, and electrical problems typically make the emergency list.

Before the contract on a major remodel is signed, homeowners should know what will happen at the end of the job. Is there a schedule for warranty items? Have it in writing.

When is the job considered "finished?" The contractor expects to be paid when the project is "substantially complete." What is "substantially complete"?

1. The agreement outlined in the contract is finished, the contractor has reached the point in the project where there is no more work that can be done, and all of the completed work is acceptable to the homeowner and/or architect.

The job is cleaned up. Establish beforehand what level of "clean" is expected. Know what the completed outside will look like. Windows washed? Will every little nail and splinter be gone from the bushes? What level of finish grading can you expect? Don't forget, most contractors aren't gardeners.

Suppose special order railings or hardware has not arrived, and you've already paid for them. A good homeowner will pay for the completed job, *including profit and overhead*, holding back only the cost of the tardy fixtures and installation labor.

Good homeowners will cut a check when the walk-thru punchlist has been completed.

2. The building department has signed off on the project, if applicable. Very important.

Mundane items, as they accumulate, should be taken care of after a few weeks have passed. Loose hardware, sticking doors, cracking grout, faulty fixtures – schedule a day when it's convenient to turn the house over to a couple of truckloads of workers and get it all done at once.

It is the responsibility of the homeowner to provide the contractor with a complete punchlist. Don't think it's OK to add items the day a crew shows up. Owners may get away adding minor stuff, (like a third or fourth small drywall touch-up) but asking a tradesman to do extra work that was not approved by the office, or requires additional ordering and scheduling, can easily create unnecessary friction among all parties. Don't assume the tile guy has a fresh tube of "Mocha Moonglow" caulk in the back of his truck, especially if you live six miles up a dirt road. Even though it's the end of the job, the potential of small problems developing into big ones still exists.

A typical home improvement contractor will offer a one year warranty on the finished product. This is a fair amount of time, because most problems usually surface within the first twelve months. Foundations and structural items usually have longer warranties. Check beforehand. Manufacturers of windows and plumbing products, for example, usually have their own warranties. Before the first year is up, make a list of any problems or issues that should be corrected or noted.

Example: *"Gutter is not pitched enough to drain towards downspout."* No one may have noticed this if the job was completed during a seasonal drought. Months later, during a big storm, it makes the list. In a perfect world, the contractor calls the gutter guys and they fix it the next time they're in the neighborhood, or within a reasonable time frame.

Provide a written record to the builder of any defects or problems, as outlined in "Problems."

Disputes at the end of the project are not inevitable, but they do occur. It is imperative to not let disagreements degenerate into a standoff where nothing gets accomplished. This is a lose-lose situation for both sides.

The contract should outline ways for disputes to be settled, and both parties need to agree with the outcome. Too many times, personalities get in the way of reason. If no provisions have been made in the contract, the Better Business Bureau is a good source for mediators.

At some point one side or another may have to make the following decision – they are dealing with a complete idiot. If this is the case, it is then imperative for the more intelligent party to protect their own interests. In the civilized world, wronged parties seek redress through the legal system, not the end of a gun barrel. Small claims court is the arena for minor disputes. Otherwise, hire a lawyer.

The cost of hiring a second contractor to complete faulty workmanship is steep. In the first place, they may be overly critical of any previous work. They know the homeowner is at a disadvantage and is anxious to find someone who can salvage their home. If a well-known Jewish carpenter didn't finish a job, it is certain the next guy along would mutter out of the corner of his mouth, "Look at this – why'd he do it this way?"

The second contractor will charge more because he may be uncertain how much is required to repair previous work, and experience makes him suspect that the homeowner is not entirely innocent in any dispute. The headache potential is a legitimate risk factor for the second contractor and can drive up the bottom line.

If disputes run amuck, the potential for disaster can cost thousands of extra dollars. Homeowners (and contractors) who remain clear headed during the remodeling process and base their decisions on reason, not emotion, have a better chance of avoiding pitfalls. Consider the preceding pages a pitfall directory.

A good remodeler has to wear a lot of hats. Aside from delivering a quality product at a fair price, remodelers need to be good listeners. Their task is to bring a client's vision to life – to fill in all the gaps of a homeowner's dream and leave them with a product that enhances their life on a constant basis.

An uninformed homeowner will be a troubled homeowner. It is incumbent upon the contractor to keep their client informed of conditions and circumstances that require immediate attention. Homeowners don't need to micro manage a project – that's the contractor's job – but do need to know when, how long, and how much. When problems arise, homeowners should understand their options.

By the same token, homeowners need to be empowered. Mississippi Man felt like he was powerless over the plumbing repairs done to his house. After dealing with a large firm on a major project, a homeowner can feel like he contracted with "HAL," the Computer, in *2001: A Space Odyssey*. Homeowners and remodelers alike must understand that major decisions that affect the construction process are, ultimately, the home-owner's responsibility. The owner hires the contractor to manage the project on a daily basis until completion, but both parties should never forget where the division of power lies. Jobs may take on a life of their own among all the subs and architects and project managers and designers and decorators. When that happens, the chances of the finished product more nearly resembling Frankenstein's monster are greatly enhanced.

Projects need to be completed. Paint needs to be touched up, invoices need to be delivered, bills must be paid, parts must (eventually) arrive, and owners must feel they have reclaimed their home and ceased to live in a construction zone. Disputes must be resolved and not left to fester. The buzzword is, "closure."

In a home, the marriage between old and new can be an awkward and uneasy fit. Worn walls are full of matronly bumps and sags, and dried out and squeaky old floors complain as they're tread upon. Some of these old houses are insulted when they learn their handsome trim is no longer available, and they hear second-hand that their wiring is frayed and sub-standard. And their plumbing! Don't talk about it!

Although they may have been the finest house in the neighborhood at one time, they may resent the intrusions and pseudo-surgery the remodeler inflicts. But a good remodeler creates a makeover that any old dowager can appreciate.

Final word: Homeowners should never make final payment to the contractor until the project has been approved by the building department...

Measure twice, cut once. Every apprentice carpenter hears this phrase. Its importance is hammered home at the end of each day by an ever-increasing pile of expensive scrap.

Many contractors start their construction careers as carpenters, and the assumption is that this mantra is forever etched in their psyche.

Billy Y____'s first solo contracting effort was beautiful. It was a "spec" house – built on the simple assumption someone would like it and then buy it. The home had tremendous curb appeal. Built at the end of the block, alongside a narrow green belt and parkway, the most prominent feature of the long two story home was a turret in the front. Perched on the turret was a jaunty rooster weather vane. Detailed filigree nestled in the gable's ends, and a wrap-around porch looked out over the green belt.

The home was primped and styled, anxious to meet her new owner. This arranged relationship could proceed when the final inspection was completed.

The final inspection is a big day in the life of a new project. A passing inspection makes everyone happy; the bankers, the builder, and the owners. Even the inspector smiles. Billy was worried about a few minor items – some of the shingles in back, he noticed long after the roofers left, should have extended a fraction of an inch more over the edge of the roof. The handrail to the basement was one of many last-minute installations, and to Billy's dismay it broke loose first thing that morning when the painter's helper pulled on it. Billy had a small mental list of little details he may have to address with the inspector, but he was proud of the place and didn't expect any major snafus.

With his Certificate of Occupancy (C.O.) in hand, he figured he could soon close a deal with one of a couple of clients who were very interested, pay everybody off, and make a little money for himself. Sure, there had been some problems and hassles along the way, but overall, he was very pleased with his initial home building effort. In another week, the noose that tightens at the end of every job was going to be off his neck.

From the kitchen he could see the inspector pull up, admire (he rightfully assumed) the finished product, and follow the walk to the front door. He knew the inspector was making sure the step to the porch landing was the correct height and the landing was the correct depth. Billy smiled knowingly as he recalled making the concrete crew move their forms another six inches toward the street just last month. The inspector looked at the step and nodded, then looked down the street to the other homes and cocked his head slightly. Then he rubbed his chin, walked back to the curb, and looked down the street again. Billy waited until the doorbell rang before he opened the door.

The project had sailed along until now. Although they weren't drinking buddies, Billy felt he had established a solid professional relationship with the inspector. So, he was surprised to see such a grim expression on the man's face before he even walked in the door.

After a cursory greeting, the inspector walked through the entry and into the front room, careful to keep his feet on the red paper pathways that had been rolled through the house. The bouquet of fresh finishes filled the bright airy rooms. Billy nervously clicked his ballpoint pen, the noise rattling through the bare rooms. The inspector studied the interior of the home as if he had never seen it before, then asked Billy to show him the "pins." The pins marked the location of the property lines. New homes are required to have a pin survey conducted, and a copy is kept on file with the building department. Billy showed him the new pins that were set in the soil by the surveyor eight months earlier, when he broke ground. This pair marked the front of the property line, and were about eight feet away from the curb.

The inspector took a deep breath before he broke the news. "Billy, you've got a major problem here. Your front easement is supposed to be twenty feet. You've only got about twelve."

The full implication didn't strike him immediately, so the inspector elaborated.

"I first noticed it when I drove up this morning and rounded the corner." The inspector walked Billy down to the green belt where they could sight down the whole block. "Look how your house is eight feet closer to the street than all the others. There's a twenty foot setback in this neighborhood, and you're just too close. Normally, we don't take a tape measure to this kind of thing, but this is major. I can't let it slide – I can't sign you off with the thing like this – what happened?"

Billy tried to collect his thoughts as his whole life practically flashed before him, and then thought back. "...I'm not really sure. When we dug the hole, I must have measured off the curb instead of the pins. I thought –"

"Well," the inspector said, "I suggest you file an appeal with Zoning and see what they say. Otherwise, you'll have to move the house back eight feet," he tried to say nonchalantly.

Billy's world had turned upside-down in a few short moments. "Eight feet!" Billy pointed toward his sprawling 3,000 square foot semi-Victorian. "How am I gonna do that? The garage backs up to the alley. It's right on the property line already!"

"Well, that's OK in the back," the inspector said. He shook his head. "I guess you'll have to take it out of the middle somewhere. Tell you what I can do."

This is the part Billy wanted to hear. If he signed him off, he would promise the inspector he would measure more carefully next time. If he wanted money, he would get it for him. In Billy's agitated state, he imagined the inspector bent over and drawers dropped. Billy would kiss his butt. Anything.

"When you get this straightened out, I won't charge a reinspection fee when it comes time for the final."

Post Mortem: The Zoning Appeals Board met once a month, and Billy couldn't plead his case for another three weeks. Subs and suppliers were sympathetic, but still anxious for their money. With the assistance of an expensive engineer, Billy spent that time concocting plan B:

The attached garage in the back was twenty-four feet long. Billy had allowed four extra feet for a workbench and a place to set groceries on before stepping up into the dining room, which led straight to the kitchen. Taking four feet out of the garage was a no-brainer. Fortunately, the house was the same width where it attached to the garage. And the garage was single story; its roof butted up against the second story.

The ceiling above the dining room was vaulted, so they supposed they could convert the spacious dining area into an eating space off the kitchen. If the appeal failed, they would have no choice.

Three weeks later Billy pleaded his case to an unsympathetic Appeals Board. They rejected his argument, and on the next day Billy began to move the front of his house back eight feet.

The project, to Billy's dismay, generated quite a bit of old-fashioned gossip in the neighborhood. Before long, crowds gawked every day and into the night at the house-moving crews that lifted the new home off its foundation and set it on massive timbers to rest three feet above grade while crews dug footings and built new foundation walls inside the existing basement. They watched in amazement as the garage was detached from the home and the slab it sat on, and its back end chopped off one afternoon like the head of a fish in the market.

The dining area was more complicated because of the wiring and and heat runs. But after stripping the drywall and siding, knocking out the brick wainscoting, and pouring some small additional foundation walls to accommodate the new location of the more expansive front of the house, they managed to rip out that pesky four extra feet in the dining room. The hardwood had to be toothed together, the floor had to be refinished, the dining room re-drywalled, and the interior repainted, especially after all the drywall cracking and nail pops from the short move. Naturally, heat ducts had to be refitted, wires rerouted, and brick replaced.

The new garage slab was torn out on one end, where it stepped up to the back of the house, and a short foundation wall was set to accommodate the new location of the existing back of the house.

Billy maxed out a couple of credit cards and used all of his imagined profits to pay for the "remodel." To add insult to injury, the new owner asked for and got a discount on the property because it had been raised, taken apart, and reassembled, as the home was not "new" anymore.

In spite of the enormous task Billy and his crews faced, they did a spectacular job cutting eight feet out of the middle of the home and piecing it back together. And the building inspector, true to his word, waived the $35 reinspection fee when Billy finally got his C.O.

When the inspector complimented him on the finished product, Billy managed a wry smile and said, "You know what they say – measure twice, cut once."

POSTSCRIPT

This book was a personal, not encyclopedic, collection of on-the-job anecdotes and problems. No notice is given to liens, foreclosures, or supercilious legal adventures. Administrative quagmires and cunumdrums of the sort that issue from local building departments are also absent.

As of this writing, I have never been the project manager of a complete disaster.

Readers who have survived and been transformed by horrible experiences in the home improvement field are eligible to contribute to *More Psychotic Remodeling*, which is already under construction. Off-beat and R-rated embarrassing moments are highly prized. If your home or job turned into a train wreck, and there's a lesson to be learned from your experience, please contact the publisher. And remember, the *Psychotic* series never reveals names and is of the firm belief that truth is stranger than fiction.

Rick MacKay

Psychotic Remodeling

ACKNOWLEDGEMENTS

Acknowledgements

I am grateful to several people whose artistic and professional talents unknowingly contributed to the final version of this book, and who still peek at me from between the lines. Edgar Allan Poe, Andreas Vesalius, Lawrence Faulkner, Auguste Rodin, James Vines, Jose Posada, John Kurowski, Pamela Colman Smith, and Rod Serling.

Psychotic Remodeling

GIVE THE GIFT OF

Psychotic Remodeling

TO YOUR
FRIENDS AND FAMILY

A GREAT GIFT FOR:

___ Dad

___ New Home Owners

___ Remodeling Victims

___ Smart Consumers

___ Contractors

___ Realtors

___ DIY'ers

___ People whose last name begins with a letter between A and Z!

CHECK YOUR LOCAL BOOKSTORE OR ORDER HERE!

Psychotic Remodeling

Order Page

ORDER PAGE

Yes I want _____Copies of *Psychotic Remodeling* for $16.99 each.

Include $3.95 shipping and handling for one book, and $1.95 for each additional book. Canadian orders must include payment in US funds, with 7% GST added. Payment must accompany orders. Allow 3 weeks for delivery.

My check or money order for $_____ is enclosed.

Please charge my   __Visa   __Mastercard   __American Express

Name _____
Organization _____
Address _____
City/State/Zip _____
Phone_____ E-mail_____
Card# _____
Exp. Date_____ Signature_____

Make your check payable and return to

Pulpville
2440 South Steele Street
Denver, CO 80210